Mistress of Hardwick

G000163349

Mistress of Hardwick

Alison Plowden

British Broadcasting Corporation

A series of 10 television programmes *Mistress of Hardwick* produced by Victor Poole. First broadcast on BBC 1 from April—June 1972.

Acknowledgment is due to the following for permission to reproduce photographs:

THE NATIONAL TRUST (photos Courtauld Institute) plates 1 and 7; R. WILSHER back cover and plates 2–6 and 8–12.

The front cover was specially photographed by Hugh Tosh.

First published 1972. Reprinted 1972

Published by the British Broadcasting Corporation
35 Marylebone High Street, London W1M 4AA
Printed in England by Cox & Wyman Ltd, London, Reading and Fakenham
ISBN: 0 563 10664 6

Contents

Author's note

This book is not a conventional biography. It grew out of the series of television programmes *Mistress of Hardwick* which set out to tell the story of that formidable woman of property, dynast and creative genius who became successively Mrs Robert Barlow, Lady Cavendish, Lady St Loe and Countess of Shrewsbury, but who is better known as Bess of Hardwick – a woman outstanding in an age of outstanding women and as renowned in her own sphere as her contemporary Queen Elizabeth.

The television series was filmed at Hardwick Hall, the only survivor of a string of houses built and re-built by Bess and which remains very much as she left it – her masterpiece and her monument. But in order to make the fullest possible use of the marvellous backdrop provided by that unique and beautiful house it was necessary, in writing the television scripts, to make use of a flashback technique, for Bess, who was not concerned with the problems of television producers and writers, did not begin to build Hardwick until she was over seventy.

In writing the book, of course, I was not circumscribed by the specialised demands and limitations of television – for example, in a series of this nature which was striving for as much authenticity as possible in background and detail, it would obviously have been self-defeating to spend too much time in locations which no longer exist. In fact, though, the book does largely follow the pattern of the scripts, but I have been able to dispense with the flashbacks and to quote some of the contemporary material at rather greater length.

In the scripts and the book I have, wherever possible, left the characters themselves to tell their story in their own words. For the television programmes we reconstructed certain dialogue scenes from the letters of the Earl of Shrewsbury, Mary Queen of Scots and her mother-in-law the Countess of Lennox, of Bess herself, her grand-daughter Arbella Stuart and many others. We made use of diaries, account books, ambassadors' despatches, the reports of spies and the depositions of prisoners. None of the named characters was invented. There is contemporary evidence for every episode. Every significant line of dialogue, every quotation used, was either written or spoken at the time in question.

Much has had to be left out. To do full justice to Bess of Hardwick would have needed twice the time and space at our disposal, but we have tried to cover the highlights of her long, eventful career. We have also tried to convey something of the flavour of the world she lived in: how it was possible for the daughter of a small squire with neither wealth nor influential relations to rise, as Bess did, by her own efforts and even to ally herself with the royal family – what was involved in building a great Elizabethan mansion like Hardwick Hall – what it cost – what sort of men did the actual work and what they were paid – how such a house was furnished – how it was run – what it looked like. We have tried, in fact, to weave into the tapestry, behind the foreground of the politics and conflicts, triumphs and tragedies of the human drama in which Bess played a leading part, some idea of what life was like at Hardwick four hundred years ago.

It would have been pretentious to include the full apparatus of notes and bibliography in a book which does not pretend to be more than a brief introduction to the subject, but the note on further reading may provide a guide to those who would like to pursue the story of Bess and her royal grand-daughter a little further.

In writing both the scripts and the book I owe a debt of gratitude to Giles Oakley, who did the research, and to Victor Poole, who planned and produced the series and who guided me patiently round the pitfalls which lie in wait for the writer coming to television for the first time. I should also like to express my appreciation to all the other members of the BBC production team whose hard work and expertise have brought the Mistress of Hardwick to life.

Alison Plowden

The Tudor, Stuart and Grey/Seymour Families

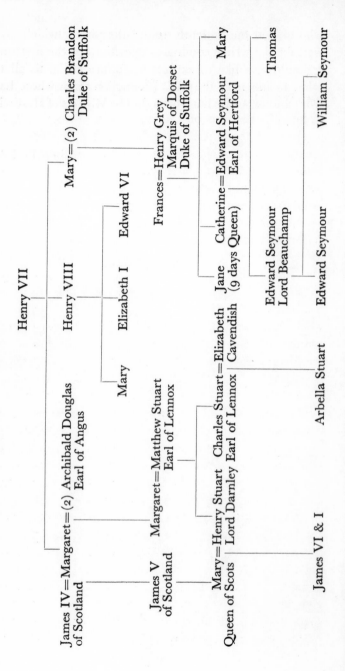

I   Honest Sweet Chatsworth

Bess was born in 1520, plain Elizabeth Hardwick, in the Old Hall, the ruins of which can still be seen from the windows of the stately mansion she built to house her dream. Although the Hardwicks had been lords of the manor for generations, they were neither rich nor important. The family led the simple, hard-working life of yeoman farmers, looking no further than their immediate neighbours for friendship and society.

Sorrow and an acquaintance with the harsh realities of life came to Bess at an early age. She was only seven when her father died and her mother was left to struggle single-handed with the problems of managing the estate and bringing-up the five children. But Mistress Hardwick would have wasted no time on self-pity. In the sixteenth century the English people were a tough, vigorous, unsentimental race, although one foreign observer thought them greedy and cold-hearted. 'The want of affection in the English is strongly manifested towards their children', wrote the author of *The Italian Relation*; 'for after having kept them at home till they arrive at the age of seven or nine years at the utmost, they put them out, both males and females, to hard service in the houses of other people. Few are born who are exempted from this fate, for everyone, however rich he may be, sends away his children into the houses of others, whilst he, in return, receives those of strangers into his own. On enquiring their reason for this severity, they answered that they did it in order that their children might learn better manners. But, for my part, I believe they do it because they like to enjoy all their comforts themselves, and are better served by strangers than they would be by their own children ... If the English sent their children away from home to learn virtue and good manners and took them back again when their apprenticeship was over, they might be excused; but they never return, for the girls are settled by their patrons, and the boys make the best marriages they can.'

Young Bess left home at the age of twelve, when Lady Zouch, a friend of the family, offered to take charge of one of the Hardwick girls. The practice of sending one's children away to be educated – always, if possible, in a household higher up the social scale than one's own – was well-established in middle- and upper-class circles, and was the fore-runner of the boarding school system which still causes foreigners some concern.

No doubt tears were shed when the actual moment of departure arrived, but as Bess helped to pack her trunk and prepared for the enormous adventure of a journey from Derbyshire to London, she would certainly not have expected to receive sympathy. At twelve years old, she would have been quite capable of realising that here might well be the chance of a lifetime, and that it was up to her to make the most of it. In an age when life itself was notoriously uncertain, childhood – for those lucky enough to survive its first few years – was not prolonged a moment longer than necessary. When Bess set out to seek her fortune, she already stood on the threshold of womanhood – a small, indomitable figure, ready to grasp whatever opportunities her world had to offer, and quite undaunted by the slenderness of her equipment.

Apart from a modest store of clothes and 'furniture' – that is, bedding and hangings – Bess was provided with a dowry of forty marks left her by her father. She had been taught to read and write, by no means a universal accomplishment, but she was not bookish by nature. In any case, the elaborate classical education just beginning to become fashionable for the daughters of the nobility was not for Bess and her sisters. By far the most important part of their training was in the practical arts of housewifery.

Richard Mulcaster, a leading educationist of the day, had no doubts on this point. 'I think it and know it', he wrote, 'to be a principal commendation in a woman to be able to govern and direct her household, to look to her house and family, to provide and keep necessaries, to know the force of her kitchen.' Mulcaster went on to say that every girl should be taught household management, and he was supported by the author of another manual on the education of young ladies. 'Our gentlewoman shall learn not only all manner of fine needlework, but whatsoever belongeth to the distaff, spindle and weaving, which must not be thought unfit for the honour and estate wherein she was born.' She should become familiar with 'the duties and offices of domestical servants' and certainly never be so proud 'that she should disdain but to be present at all household works'.

It is not likely that Bess was ever allowed to disdain to be present at any household chore, and by the time she left home she would have learnt to bake and brew, to spin and weave, been initiated into the mysteries of the herb-garden and still-room, been taught the elements of butter and cheese making and how to care for the poultry yard. All her training would, in fact, have been directed towards preparing her for the only career open to a respectable woman, that of being the mistress of her own household – a demanding, responsible and highly-skilled occupation in the days when all the necessities of daily life, from food and drink to clothes and medicines, had to be grown or made at home and every self-respecting manor or farmhouse prided itself on being self-sufficient.

To a country-bred girl like Bess her first sight of London must have come as something of a shock. The Tudor city, still bounded by its Roman and mediaeval walls, was a congested, noisy, insanitary place. Open drains ran down the middle of narrow streets, lined with tall wooden houses, clamorous with apprentices crying their masters' wares, crowded with herds of cattle being driven to market, strings of pack-horses laden with produce, porters pushing barrows or carrying bundles on their heads, shoppers intent on a bargain, visitors, sightseers, foreign sailors and merchants.

Bess never really took to town life, but she soon fulfilled the hopes of her well-wishers by finding herself a husband – young Robert Barlow, also from Derbyshire and also a member of Lady Zouch's household. Years later, when Nathaniel Johnston was writing the life of the Earl of Shrewsbury, he thought it worthwhile to include the story of the Countess's first marriage.

'I have been informed by some ancient gentlemen that it was accomplished by her being at London attending the Lady Zouch at such time as Mr Barlow lay sick there of a chronical distemper. In which time this young gentlewoman making him many visits, upon account of their neighbourhood in the country and out of kindness to him, being very solicitous to afford him all help she was able to do in his sickness, ordering his diet and attendance, being young and very handsome, he fell deeply in love with her, of whose great affections to her she made such advantage, that for lack of issue by her, he settled a large inheritance in lands upon her and her heirs, which by his death she fully enjoyed.'

In the circumstances it is not surprising that Robert Barlow should have fallen in love with Bess, but the sixteenth century took the same severely practical view of matrimony as of everything else. Nine out of ten marriages were arranged between families with an eye to financial or social advancement, although the 'free and full' consent of the young people concerned was regarded as a necessary condition. Forced marriages did sometimes take place, but they were generally frowned upon. Equally, of course, children who married without their parents' consent, were considered to have 'grievously offended'. Robert and Bess don't appear to have had any opposition to contend with. Mistress Hardwick would have been delighted to see her daughter so creditably established, while the Barlows may have felt that despite the smallness of her dowry, a healthy, energetic, well-brought-up girl like Bess would be just the wife for their delicate son.

When Bess embarked on married life she would have had a voluminous literature on the subject at her disposal. Every writer on the perennially fascinating topic of marriage was agreed that a wife's first duty was to obey her husband in everything 'not repugnant to honesty'. She must always be merry and cheerful in his presence, 'but yet not with too much lightness'. If he rebuked her unfairly, she must bear it patiently. She should be seen rather than heard, for a silent woman was regarded as a treasure. She must be very careful of her good name and not always wanting to go gadding about. In theory, she should only leave her home to go to church or perhaps to assist one of her neighbours at a lying-in, and certainly she should never go out without her husband's permission. Needless to say, the purveyors of all this good advice were men, and in practice a sensible woman would soon learn to manage her husband to her own satisfaction. One cynical writer observed that 'women are called night-crows, for that commonly in the night they will make request for such toys as cometh into their heads in the day. Women know their time to work their craft; for in the night they will work a man like wax, and draw him like as Adamant doth Iron.' This was the moment to ask for 'a gown of the new fashion', for a new petticoat or for a hat of the latest fashion. The husband would yield, partly because he was overcome by 'her flattering speech' and partly 'because he would sleep quietly in his bed'.

Robert Barlow's bride had little opportunity to employ such time-honoured tactics, for the sickly boy died in February, 1533, within a few months of their marriage.

As a young, attractive widow with money of her own Bess would not have lacked for suitors, but evidently she enjoyed her independence too much to give it up lightly. There is no record of her life for the next fourteen years, but most probably she went back to Derbyshire to look after the property Robert had left her, which included timber, lead mines and agricultural land. These quiet years may have laid the foundations of her robust good health and astonishing longevity. She had married young, even by the standards of her time, but unlike so many of her contemporaries, she was not exhausted and prematurely aged by continuous child-bearing in her teens and early twenties.

When Bess did marry again, she chose well. Her second husband was Sir William Cavendish, who had been one of the Royal Commissioners employed in the business of dissolving the monasteries and who, in company with most of his colleagues, had done very nicely out of it. He had been granted some church lands as a reward for his services and been able to buy others cheaply. In 1541 he was sent over to Ireland to make a survey of monastic property there and earned a glowing testimonial from the Lord Deputy. Five years later, William Cavendish was knighted and made Treasurer of the King's Chamber. When he courted Bess in 1547, he was a prosperous and highly respected figure. The fact that he was at least fifteen years her senior and already had eight children by previous marriages in no way detracted from his eligibility. Their wedding took place on August 20th at Bradgate, the home of Henry Grey, Marquis of Dorset, at the somewhat eccentric hour of two o'clock in the morning. Sir William was a friend of the Marquis, soon to become Duke of Suffolk, and his wife Frances, niece of Henry VIII and mother of Jane Grey. It is possible that Bess may have been occupying some position in the household and that she met William Cavendish there.

The marriage turned out both happy and successful. Within a year Bess's first child was born, a daughter christened Frances. Another daughter, Temperance, born in 1549, failed to survive but three sturdy sons, Henry, William and Charles, soon arrived to fill the gap. Then came Elizabeth, Mary and finally Lucrece, born in March, 1557. Lucrece also died in infancy, but to have reared six babies out of eight was an achievement to be proud of.

By the time the last two children were born, the Cavendishes were spending most of their time in Derbyshire. As Protestants in the reign of the Catholic Mary Tudor, they would have found it wiser to keep away from Court – especially after the abortive *coup d'état* of 1553 which had brought disaster to their friends the Duke and Duchess of Suffolk and the pathetic nine days Queen, Lady Jane Grey. Bess had plenty to keep her busy in the country. As well as raising her young family, she had begun to indulge her passion for building. In 1549, she and Sir William had acquired the house and estate of Chatsworth, about fifteen miles from Hardwick. The house was in a very bad state of repair, but to begin with Bess contented herself with renovations. She paid Master Bisseter, a carpenter 'for himself and his man for working at Chatsworth by the space of seventy-two days at eightpence the day for himself and fivepence the day for his man'. Small sums were also spent on mending doors and locks. All the same, Chatsworth evidently remained a pretty uncomfortable place, for in 1552 Bess was writing to her steward, Francis Whitfield: 'Cause the floor in my bedchamber to be made even, either with plaster, clay or lime, and all the windows where the glass is broken to be mended and all the chambers to be made as close and warm as you can.' But by this time plans for a fine new house had been drawn up by the mason, Roger Worth. No trace now remains of Bess's Chatsworth, but following the fashion of the time, it was grouped round a central courtyard, the entrance being through an archway between turrets in the middle of one side – the hall, buttery and kitchen running along the opposite side.

William Cavendish took a close interest in the progress of the work and in March, 1555, he addressed an appeal to his friend, Sir John Thynne, who was also building down in the West Country. 'Sir, I understand that you have a cunning plasterer at Longleat, which hath in your hall and in other places of your house made divers pendants and other pretty things. If your business be at an end, or will be by next summer after this, I would pray you that I might have him in Derbyshire, for my hall is yet unmade. And therefore now might he devise with my own carpenter how he should frame the same that it might serve for his work.'

In 1557 all these cheerful plans were tragically interrupted. That August Sir William was in London on business, when Bess heard that he'd been taken seriously ill. She set off at once from Chatsworth, making a succession of forced marches to reach him. Even so, the journey took four days and three nights. On the first day a guide was necessary, so bad was the state of the roads, and at St Albans an armed guard of four men had to be hired at a cost of ten shillings to protect the party from the dangers of travel by night.

Bess nursed William Cavendish with as much devotion as once she had nursed Robert Barlow. All sorts of delicacies were tried to tempt the appetite of the invalid, including necks of mutton, pigeons, oysters, whiting, capons and calves foot jelly. But it was no use. Two months later Bess opened the pocket book in which Sir William had carefully recorded the details of their marriage and the births and christenings of their children, and made a sad little entry of her own: 'Sir William Cavendish, knight, my most dear and well-beloved husband, departed this present life on Monday, being the

25th day of October, betwixt the hours of eight and nine of the same day at night, in the year of our Lord God, 1557. On whose soul I most humbly beseech the Lord to have mercy and to rid me and his poor children out of our great misery.'

Bess and William Cavendish had been ideally suited and she mourned him sincerely. Nevertheless, her second widowhood was much shorter than her first – she had the future of her six small children to consider now. In 1559 she married Sir William St Loe, another widower much older than herself with children of his own. St Loe was scarcely a romantic figure but he, too, was a wealthy landowner and could certainly be regarded as a good match from the worldly point of view. As it turned out, Bess had once more chosen well. William St Loe proved the most generous and loving of husbands. He showed no jealousy over her absorption in her building activities – indeed he once began a letter to her as 'my honest sweet Chatsworth'. At other times she was 'my own sweet Bess . . . more dearer to me than I am to myself'.

Her marriage to St Loe brought Bess to Court for the first time, and at a particularly exciting time. Sad Mary Tudor was dead and now a new Queen, the young red-headed, imperious Elizabeth was letting a gust of fresh air and optimism into a country heartily sick of weak, factious government, internal dissension and bad housekeeping. The St Loes were in a privileged position. Sir William had shown himself a good friend to Elizabeth at a time when she had been in great danger, and she had rewarded him by making him Captain of the Guard and Butler to the Royal Household. Bess became one of the ladies of the Privy Chamber, but she was soon to discover that no one, however privileged, was immune from the dangers which lurked at Courts.

Trouble for Lady St Loe took the shape of some highly unwelcome confidences from Lady Catherine Grey, younger sister of the unfortunate Jane and now, by the terms of Henry VIII's Will, heiress presumptive to the throne. Throughout the summer of 1561 the matrons of the Court had been casting increasingly suspicious glances at Lady Catherine, and early in August she sought Bess out to confess that she had been secretly married the previous autumn to the Earl of Hertford and was now pregnant. Distraught and frightened, she begged Lady St Loe to help her break the news to the Queen, but although Catherine Grey's mother had been her friend and Catherine was godmother to one of her children, Bess could not or would not allow herself the luxury of kindness to the forlorn girl of twenty, now very near her time. The risks attached to becoming involved in the royal family's affairs were well-known and Bess, breaking into 'a passion of weeping', hastily dissociated herself from Lady Catherine's troubles. But Lady Catherine's condition could no longer be ignored and a few days after her appeal to Bess the storm broke.

Anything which affected the succession, even indirectly, touched the Queen on her most sensitive spot. She had not forgotten – she was never to forget – her own experiences as a 'second person' during the reign of her sister Mary and of the intrigues which inevitably surrounded the heir to the Throne. In the activities of the present heir she had caught a sulphurous whiff of treason and Catherine Grey and her young husband were promptly arrested. Even in her twenties Elizabeth Tudor was a formidable figure – as one ambassador remarked, 'she gives her orders and has her way as absolutely as her father did' – and soon further orders reached Sir Edward Warner, Lieutenant of the Tower. 'You shall send for St Loe', wrote the Queen, 'and put her in awe of divers matters confessed by the Lady Catherine, and so also deal with her that she may confess to you all her knowledge in the same matter.'

Elizabeth was convinced that there was more to Catherine Grey's secret marriage than met the eye – nor was her temper improved when Catherine presently gave birth to a healthy son. It is a little difficult to believe that Bess, with her close connections with the Grey family, had had no inkling of what had been going on, but no evidence of her complicity ever came to light. Even so, she spent seven months in the Tower – an unnerving experience and a sharp warning never to meddle in affairs of state.

Three years after her release, she became a widow for the third time. William St Loe had made a Will leaving her all his property, but Bess had to face a good deal of unpleasantness from the St Loe family, who were under-standably aggrieved and some ugly accusations of poison-ing and witchcraft were bandied about. Bess was now forty-four, self-confident, strong-willed and still very handsome with her slender, upright figure, reddish hair and fine complexion. An efficient businesswoman, she managed her large estates with 'masculine understanding' and kept an unforgiving eye on every detail, every sub-ordinate. She was by this time a wealthy woman and a matrimonial prize in her own right, and there was a good deal of speculation as to who her next husband would be. The names of Sir John Thynne, the builder of Longleat, Lord Darcy and Lord Cobham were all mentioned. But Bess was in no hurry. It was not until 1568 that she made her last and most brilliant marriage, to George Talbot, sixth Earl of Shrewsbury – yet another widower with children of his own, yet another extremely rich man with property all over the north of England. It seemed as if everything Bess touched turned to gold. Her enemies did not hesitate to accuse her of an insatiable lust for power and wealth, but much of her driving ambition was now centred on her children. Before she accepted Shrewsbury, she insisted that her eldest son, Henry Cavendish, and her youngest daughter, Mary, should be married to his eldest daughter and second son, Gilbert Talbot. To mark this auspicious occasion, Bess ordered a walnut table to be made, inlaid with chessmen, dice and musical instruments, with the Talbot arms impaled by those of the Cavendish family – a table which stands today in the High Presence Chamber at Hardwick Hall.

Yet again it seemed as if Bess was to be lucky in love, for George Talbot had fallen completely under the spell of her powerful personality. Queen Elizabeth was graciously pleased to approve the marriage – the Catherine Grey episode had now been forgiven and forgotten – and Her Majesty was heard to remark: 'I have been glad to see my lady St Loe, but now more desirous to see my lady Shrewsbury. I hope my lady hath known my good opinion of her . . . There is no lady in this land that I better love and like.'

Bess had come a long way since that day, more than a quarter of a century earlier, when she had set out for London with no assets beyond her youth and optimism, and a dowry of not quite twenty-seven pounds. The past had been astonishingly successful. The future looked comfortably assured. When Lady St Loe went to the altar with the Earl of Shrewsbury, there was nothing but her own restless spirit to warn her of the storms which lay ahead.

2   Dangerous Alliance

In one of the turrets of Hardwick Hall there is a small room dedicated to the memory of Mary Queen of Scots, with her arms blazoned over the door. Mary had gone to her death in the Great Hall of Fotheringay Castle four years before the new Hardwick began to rise from its foundations, and why this room was furnished with relics of the tragic Queen, or who furnished it, remains a mystery. Bess did not refer to it as the 'Scots Room' in the inventory of Hardwick which she herself compiled in 1601, yet she had every reason to remember her long association with Mary Stuart – an association which had brought her and her posterity nothing but disappointment and heartbreak.

At about the same time that Bess became Countess of Shrewsbury, the Queen of Scots, deposed and imprisoned by her ungrateful subjects, was making her spectacular escape from Lochleven Castle. Her hopes of regaining the Scottish throne by force of arms were quickly dashed and a few days later she crossed the Solway Firth in a fishing boat to seek sanctuary in England – a fugitive with nothing in the world but the clothes she stood up in. Sir Francis Knollys, who was hastily despatched to Carlisle to take charge of this unusual refugee, found her surprisingly undaunted by her misfortunes. 'This lady and princess is a notable woman', he wrote to his friend William Cecil. 'She seemeth to regard no ceremonious honour beside the acknowledging of her estate regal. She showeth a disposition to speak much, to be bold, to be pleasant, and to be very familiar. She showeth a great desire to be avenged of her enemies ... The thing that most she thirsteth after is victory, and it seemeth to be indifferent to her to have her enemies diminished either by the sword of her friends, or by the liberal promises and rewards of her purse, or by division and quarrels raised among themselves; so that for victory's sake, pain and peril seemeth pleasant unto her, and in respect of victory, wealth and all things seem to her contemptible and vile. Now what is to be done with such a lady and princess?'

What indeed. This was a question which Queen Elizabeth and her Council were to ask themselves repeatedly during the next eighteen years. As the grand-daughter of Henry VIII's elder sister, Mary Stuart had an undeniable right to be recognised as Elizabeth's heir. Catholics, both native and European, thought she had every right to be recognised as Queen of England without further delay. The English government, therefore, faced a virtually insoluble problem. Mary had powerful friends abroad, and to let her go free would have been to invite disaster. They could not in decency hand her back to the Scots, who would have made short work of her. On the other hand, as the historian William Camden sagely observed: 'If she were detained in England, they reasoned lest she (who was as it were the very pith and marrow of sweet eloquence) might draw many daily to her part which favoured her title to the Crown of England, who would kindle the coals of her ambition, and leave nothing unassayed whereby they might set the crown upon her head.'

These fears turned out to be only too well founded, but as long as Mary was kept a prisoner in England her movements could at least be controlled and her activities watched. Given the circumstances, the choice of custodian was obviously of paramount importance. He must be incorruptible; conscientious enough to be willing to accept such a thankless task; rich enough to be able to bear the expense such an 'honour' would be bound to entail, and preferably in a position to provide suitable accommodation for his charge. In December, 1568 Queen Elizabeth began to drop hints to the Earl of Shrewsbury, 'declaring that ere it were long I should well perceive she did so trust me as she did few'. 'She would not tell me wherein', wrote the Earl to his new wife, 'but doubt it was about the custody of the Scots Queen.' A little later Bess heard from one of her nephews in London: 'The news is here that my lord your husband is sworn of the Privy Council and that the Scottish Queen is on her journey to Tutbury, something against her will, and will be under my lord's custody there.'

Tutbury Castle in Staffordshire was Crown property leased by the Shrewsburys, who used it as a hunting box. As a prison it had the advantage of being easily defensible. As a country residence in the depth of winter it had little to recommend it – being damp, bitterly cold and half ruined. The task of making Tutbury habitable at virtually a moment's notice was a challenge to her housekeeping abilities and Bess rose to the occasion with her usual efficiency. 'The house being unready in many respects for the receiving of the Scottish Queen coming at such a sudden', she wrote, 'I have caused workmen to make forthwith in readiness all things as are most needful to be done before her coming, and, God willing, I shall cause three or four lodgings to be furnished with hangings and other necessaries.' Rather than she should not 'with true and faithful heart answer the trust reposed by the Queen's Majesty' declared Bess, she would go without 'furniture of lodging' for herself.

Shrewsbury had wanted to take the Queen of Scots to his own house, Sheffield Castle, where there would have been more room for the large retinue of servants she had now acquired. But by the time the Council in London agreed to this, all the best tapestries and Turkey carpets had been moved to Tutbury and it was too late to change the plan. Conditions were certainly crowded and uncomfortable for the two households, but Mary had a suite of three rooms – a great chamber, an outer chamber and an inner chamber – and apart from the cold and damp, which was the same for everybody, the worst she had to suffer was the boredom and frustration of captivity. The weather made any form of outdoor exercise impossible, and Nicholas White, a visitor at Tutbury, asked her how she passed her time. 'She said that all the day she wrought with her needle, and that the diversity of the colours made the work seem less tedious, and continued so long at it till very pain made her to give over, and with that laid her hand upon her left side, and complained of an old grief newly increased there.'

Mary, who had driven her first guardian, Francis Knollys, to desperation by her tantrums, never made any secret of the fact that she hated Tutbury, but all the same, the first few months she spent in the Earl of Shrewsbury's care passed comparatively peacefully. This was partly due to the friendship she had struck up with Bess. 'This Queen continueth daily resort unto my wife's chamber', reported the Earl, 'where with the Lady Leviston and Mrs Seaton, she sits working with the needle, in which she much delights, and devising of further works.' Shrewsbury was able to reassure the Council that 'her talk is altogether of indifferent and trifling matters, without any sign of secret dealing or practice'.

They made a strange pair: the exquisitely feminine Queen of Scots, already at twenty-seven a figure of romantic legend, and shrewd successful Bess of Hardwick the yeoman's daughter, nearly fifty now, who had doggedly fought and married her way up the social ladder. And yet they had a surprising amount in common. Both were skilful, enthusiastic needlewomen. Both had a discerning eye for beautiful surroundings and a developed taste in luxury. Both possessed devious and scheming brains. No doubt much of the time they spent together was occupied in discussing designs for their next set of cushions, bed curtains or wall hangings: Mary employed a professional embroiderer who was able to draw patterns for the ladies and fill in the boring bits of background for them. The Queen of Scots would also have been in a position to advise Bess, who was still busy building Chatsworth, on the latest styles in interior decoration. This was women's chatter, which the careful Shrewsbury could safely dismiss as trifling, but there must have been occasions when their talk turned to other, more dangerous, topics.

The reason publicly advanced by Queen Elizabeth for keeping Mary under restraint and refusing to receive her at Court was that the Queen of Scots still lay under grave suspicion of having been an accessory before the fact of the murder of her second husband, Henry Stuart Lord Darnley. It would surely be strange if, during those long intimate sessions over the embroidery frames, Bess did not hear – more than once – Mary's side of the story. Mary had flatly refused to testify, even by proxy, at the special tribunal which Elizabeth had set up to enquire into the dispute between the Queen of Scots and her subjects. It was not for her, a sovereign princess, to justify herself before her own rebels. It was the Scottish lords, Mary maintained, who had secretly slain her husband and destroyed the house at Kirk o'Field 'so that scarce one stone was left standing upon another'. The assassination of Darnley had really been an attempt on her own life, she declared, and when it had failed, her enemies had accused her of being guilty of the crime. They had dishonoured her, forced her to abdicate and made her good subjects hate her. They held her infant son a prisoner, had threatened to put her to death and had even stolen her rings and jewels. Mary would have been only too pleased to answer their wicked slanders before Elizabeth, 'as one friend, one princess, to another'. She would never answer to anyone else. Nor would she speak while she remained in prison. She could not understand why the Queen of

England, 'her good sister', apparently preferred to believe the word of rebels and traitors rather than that of her own kinswoman and cousin.

While Bess sat listening with half an ear to the Queen of Scots expatiating on her grievances, it seems as if an idea gradually began to take shape in her mind. She spent more and more of her time in Mary's company. Was she perhaps brooding quietly on the ramifications of the Tudor and Stuart families? Lord Darnley, who had died violently in the house at Kirk o'Field, had been Mary's first cousin as well as her husband. Darnley was dead, but he had a younger brother, Charles, now in his early teens. After Mary Queen of Scots and her little son James, Charles Stuart could lay legitimate claim to the thrones of England and Scotland. Mary was a prisoner, constantly complaining how ill she felt. James was a mere baby in the hands of the Scottish war-lords – his future looked uncertain to put it mildly. But Charles Stuart was in England, still in the care of his widowed mother, the Countess of Lennox. And Bess had a daughter still unmarried. The seed of a plan more ambitious, more far-reaching in its implications than anything she had yet attempted, germinated slowly. There was no hurry. Bess was content to wait and watch.

In the autumn of 1574, the Countess of Lennox left London to visit her estates in Yorkshire, taking her son Charles with her. On their way north they made an overnight stop at Huntingdon to stay with an old friend, the Dowager Duchess of Suffolk, now married to Mr Bertie. By a strange coincidence the Countess of Shrewsbury happened to be at Rufford, one of the many Shrewsbury houses in the neighbourhood. By an even more curious coincidence she had chosen to ride over to see *her* old friend, Mrs Bertie. It would be fascinating to know what these three formidable matrons found to talk about that evening. It was clearly a satisfactory encounter, for Bess issued a pressing invitation to the Lennoxes to spend a few days at Rufford before continuing their journey. Unfortunately, though, no sooner had mother and son arrived at Rufford than Lady Lennox fell ill. As a good hostess and notable sick nurse, Bess naturally devoted herself to the invalid. Her daughter, nineteen-year-old Elizabeth Cavendish, was left to entertain Charles Stuart and for a brief, halcyon period romance blossomed and burgeoned in the gardens of the old Cistercian Abbey of Rufford.

According to the Earl of Shrewsbury's account of the matter: 'The Lady Lennox, being as I hear sickly, rested her at Rufford five days and kept most her chamber, and in that time the young man her son fell into liking with my wife's daughter before intended. And such liking was between them as my wife tells me she makes no doubt of a match.' In fact, by the time the two mothers emerged from the sick room, they apparently found there was nothing else for it. The young couple had 'so tied themselves together upon their own liking as they cannot be parted', wrote Shrewsbury, 'and the young man is so far in love that belike he is sick without her'. It seemed that there were few noblemen's sons in England that Bess had not prayed her husband 'to deal for' at one time or another on her daughter's behalf, 'and now' he assured Lord Burghley, 'this comes unlooked for and without thanks to me'.

The betrothal of Charles Stuart and Elizabeth Cavendish may have been no thanks to the Earl of Shrewsbury. Whether it came entirely unlooked for is another matter altogether. Elizabeth was a gentle, affectionate girl who, until now, had been unaccountably disappointed in the various marriage plans suggested for her – nineteen was a ripe age to be still a spinster. Thrown into the company of a good-looking and eligible young man, it is hardly surprising that she should have succumbed. A Cavendish could scarcely be regarded as an equal match for a royal

Stuart, but although Charles possessed a full share of the family charm he also showed signs of developing some of the less attractive traits which had been so conspicuous in his elder brother. Lady Lennox may have been quite simply delighted that her difficult son had fallen in love with a nice girl like Elizabeth Cavendish. There may have been other considerations. The Lennoxes were chronically short of money and the evidence of Shrewsbury and Cavendish wealth clearly visible around them, cannot have failed to tempt. Besides this, Bess could be very persuasive when she chose.

Elizabeth and Charles were married very quietly at Rufford that autumn – so quietly, in fact, that it was nearly a month before Queen Elizabeth heard about it. When she did, she was furious and the Earl of Shrewsbury hastily took up his pen again to write to Lord Burghley. 'My very good lord, I am advertised the late marriage of my wife's daughter is not well taken in the Court, and thereupon are some conjectures brought to Her Majesty's ears in ill part against my wife . . . If your lordship meet with anything thereof that concerns my wife or me, and sounds in ill part against us, let me crave of your lordship so much favour as to speak your knowledge and opinion of us both.'

The newly-weds and their respective mothers had been ordered to present themselves in London without delay, but winter had set in by this time and the shocking state of the roads gave the culprits an excuse for prolonging their journey. The Countess of Lennox, forced to stay for a few days at Huntingdon to rest herself and her 'over-laboured mules', appealed to the Earl of Leicester for his intercession. Lady Lennox knew she was in serious trouble. There seemed only one note to strike and she struck it hard. 'Now, my lord, for that hasty marriage of my son Charles. After that he had entangled himself so that he could have none other, I refer the same to your lordship's good consideration, whether it was not most fitting for me to marry them, he being mine only son and comfort that is left me.'

The succession was still an extremely sensitive political issue. By their match-making activities Bess and Lady Lennox had trespassed on forbidden ground, inviting the Queen's wrath and all the disastrous consequences which that could bring with it. The Earl of Shrewsbury, unable to leave his charge, now at Sheffield Castle, was only too well aware of this and continued to bombard Burghley, Leicester and the Queen herself with exculpatory letters. 'May it please your Majesty, I understand of late your Majesty's displeasure is sought against my wife, for marriage of her daughter to my Lady Lennox's son. I must confess to your Majesty, as true it is, it was dealt in suddenly, and without my knowledge; but, as I dare undertake and ensure to your Majesty, for my wife, she finding her daughter disappointed . . . and that the young gentleman was inclined to love with a few days' acquaintance, did her best to further her daughter to this match without having therein any other intent or respect than with reverend duty towards your Majesty.'

It all sounded pretty thin. This affecting story of whirlwind romance was hardly likely to impress the Queen, who was well-known to regard such lack of self-control with a notably cold and unforgiving eye. However, it was Shrewsbury's story and he was sticking to it.

In spite of bad roads, flooded roads, in some places no roads at all, the two Countesses reached London by about December 12th and Lady Lennox addressed a final plaintive appeal to Lord Leicester from her house at Hackney. 'And surely, my lord, touching the marriage, other dealing or longer practice there was none, but the sudden affection of my son. Therefore, I beg your lordship to be a means unto her Majesty to pity my cause and painful travel, and to have compassion on my widowed state, being aged and of many cares.'

All this time the chief culprit had been maintaining a stony silence. No lame excuses, no pleas for forgiveness or protestations of innocence were heard from Bess. If she had deliberately engineered a marriage between her daughter and one of Queen Elizabeth's closest relatives without the Queen's knowledge or consent – and it looks very much as though she had done just that – then she had been asking for trouble. After her unpleasant experience at the time of the long dead Catherine Grey's secret marriage, no one should have known that better than Bess herself. Possibly she was gambling on the fact that the government would find it too embarrassing to press charges against the wife of Mary Queen of Scots' custodian. At any rate, she obviously felt the less she said the better. On December 27th the blow fell and she and Lady Lennox were sent to cool their heels in the Tower while their actions were minutely investigated.

No record appears to have survived of the examination of the ladies themselves, but Francis Walsingham drew up a significant list of questions to be put to Thomas Fowler, Lady Lennox's steward.

'Whether about midsummer last he was not sent to his mistress's house at Templenewsam.

'If he was, for what cause.

'Whether during his being at Templenewsam he went to speak to Lady Shrewsbury . . .

'Whether about midsummer last he knew, or at least had some conjecture, of the marriage between Charles Stuart and Lady Shrewsbury's daughter . . .'

But it was not, of course, the marriage alone which was causing Queen Elizabeth and her Council so much concern. The question they really wanted answered was whether this convenient 'romance' perhaps concealed yet another plot in favour of Mary Stuart. According to the French ambassador, 'the Queen of Scots is so subjected to calumnies, and her enemies are so prompt in attributing to her all the ills and disorders which happen in this realm, that they have even persuaded this Queen (Elizabeth) that she is the cause of the marriage between Charles, Earl of Lennox, and Elizabeth Cavendish, daughter of the Countess of Shrewsbury, and that she had leagued the Duchess of Suffolk and the Countess of Lennox with the said Countess of Shrewsbury to do many things for her in this realm. On the contrary, the Queen of Scotland fears more than anything in the world the colleaguing together of these three ladies (two of whom have always been her decided enemies). She is above all convinced that it will lead to her being roughly torn from the keeping of the Earl of Shrewsbury and consigned to those whom she suspects of seeking her death.'

The Countess of Lennox had blamed Mary bitterly for being the murderess of her son, Lord Darnley, and it did not, on the face of it, seem very likely that she would go out of her way to help her former daughter-in-law. All the same, the dangerous possibility of a reconciliation between them remained in Elizabeth's mind. As for Bess, her friendship with the Queen of Scots had not gone unobserved. But if Bess had been in collusion with Lady Lennox to arrange the marriage of their son and daughter, she had successfully covered her tracks. The whole affair is a little mysterious. What had prompted Bess to take such an enormous risk? Had she really planned it all in advance, or was it the sudden, spur of a moment seizing of an opportunity? Most surprising of all, why did she get away with it? It appears that once the government were satisfied that no plot involving Mary Queen of Scots could be traced back to Bess or Lady Lennox they rather lost interest. Lady Lennox was kept in the Tower until the autumn of 1575, but Bess, unscathed and still apparently unrepentant, was back in Derbyshire in good time for the birth of her grandchild.

The baby was a girl, christened Arbella – an unusually fanciful choice among so many Elizabeths, Marys and Margarets – amid all the pomp and ceremony proper to such an important occasion. After the child had been sprinkled with consecrated water from the font, the sponsors placed their hands on it and the minister covered it with a white vestment called the chrysom – a token of innocence. The baby was then anointed (a relic of the Catholic service), the godparents offered their gifts of gold and silver plate, and refreshments of wafers, comfits and spiced wine were brought into the church. Then the procession formed up to return to the great house – Arbella was in all probability born at Chatsworth and christened in the parish church of Edensor close by – and the rest of the day was given over to feasting and festivity.

If Bess had been disappointed by the baby's sex, she gave no sign of it. It was enough that she had a grand-child of the blood royal. She herself could expect no further advancement but now her fame and her un-quenchable ambition would live on in a third generation. She had gambled a great deal on a single throw. She had survived. She had achieved her immediate objective. Who could tell what the future might hold for the house of Stuart and of Cavendish?

3 *My Jewel Arbelle*

The birth of Arbella Stuart was to change Bess's whole outlook, giving her new purpose and direction, a new interest in the future. At fifty-five – an age when many of her contemporaries regarded their useful lives as being virtually at an end – Bess was able to look forward to the absorbing task of preparing her grand-daughter to be worthy of a splendid destiny – to be worthy, in fact, to succeed Queen Elizabeth on the English throne.

The Elizabethans were not given to sentimentality over their children. Childhood was looked upon as a tiresome but unavoidable delay in reaching profitable adult life and one which for everybody's sake should be got over as quickly as possible. Bess was perhaps the least sentimental of her generation, but there was pleasure as well as solid satisfaction in watching the baby Arbella grow into a sturdy, fair-haired toddler, taking her first uncertain steps in the galleries and gardens of Chatsworth, Hardwick Old Hall or Sheffield Castle, and rapidly developing into 'a very proper child'. 'She is of very great towardness to learn anything', wrote Bess, imperfectly concealing her grandmotherly pride, 'and I very careful of her good education, as if she were my own and only child, and a great deal more for the nearness of blood she is in to her Majesty.'

Arbella owed her very existence to Bess's talents as a match-maker and such an important little girl must obviously make a brilliant marriage herself. Not even the Countess of Shrewsbury could embark on negotiations with foreign royalty, but looking nearer home there was one especially promising candidate. 'A friend in office', observed Lord Paget in a letter to the Earl of Northumberland, 'is very desirous that the Queen should have light given her of the practice between Leicester and the Countess for Arbella, for it comes on very lustily, insomuch as the said Earl hath sent down a picture of his baby.'

The Earl of Leicester's son Robert, 'the noble impe', was not yet three years old, but the betrothals of children of nursery age were by no means unusual in royal and noble families. A betrothal or spousal – that is, a promise to marry made in the present tense before witnesses was held to be a legal and binding contract. The same promise given in the future tense, *'in verbis de futuro'*, was a rather different matter. This form of betrothal, generally carried out by proxy, was little more than a conditional statement of intent to have a marriage performed at some future date. Portraits and suitably expensive presents were exchanged and, if the children concerned were old enough, formal letters dictated by tutors expressing undying affection; but in fact a ceremony of this kind had no binding force on either side. In the case of little Robert and Arbella any such contract was soon broken with grim finality by the death of the 'noble impe'. Bess made no more marriage plans. She may well have been given a private but unmistakable warning not to try again. At any rate, she now concentrated all her energies on bringing up her grand-daughter as nearly as possible in imitation of the Queen herself.

Elizabeth's principal tutor had been Roger Ascham, Fellow of St John's College and most famous of the bright young men who had gathered at Cambridge in the early years of the century. Ascham held advanced ideas on education and the Princess Elizabeth had made great strides under his supervision. 'She speaks French and Italian as well as she does English', he had written of his famous pupil, 'and has often talked to me readily and well in Latin, moderately well in Greek. She read with me almost the whole of Cicero and a great part of Livy. From these two authors her knowledge of the Latin language has been almost exclusively derived. The beginning of the day was always devoted to the New Testament in Greek, after which she read select orations of Isocrates and the tragedies of Sophocles.' Ascham taught Elizabeth by his famous method of double translation, presenting her with a passage of Latin or Greek to be first turned into English and then translated back into the original; a method which was probably copied by Arbella's tutors.

Formal education began early. The general age of entry into grammar school was six or seven, by which time the 'pettys', as they were called, were expected to be able to read and write and say their Catechism. Like Elizabeth, Arbella studied modern languages as well as the classics, but few children shared her opportunities. The business of the grammar schools – backbone of the educational system – was to teach Latin, still an essential tool for anyone contemplating a professional career in the Church, law, medicine or government service. English was not yet thought of as a separate subject, and any knowledge of English grammar had to be picked up while learning Latin. The same applied to history and geography. Arithmetic was an extra – taught on Saturdays and half-holidays, which doubtless did not add to its appeal.

Although the drudgery of parsing, construing and learning rules by rote was occasionally relieved by the performance of a Greek or Latin play, education was regarded as a serious business. The Elizabethans did not expect their sons to find it pleasant. School hours were long – from six or seven in the morning till eleven, and again from one o'clock to four or five in the afternoon – and discipline was harsh, sometimes brutal, so that 'many young wits were driven to hate learning before they knew what learning was'. Girls' schools were still unknown. The fashion for learned women, born out of the Renaissance enthusiasm for knowledge for its own sake, affected only a very small group, with royal ladies in the forefront.

While Arbella was imbibing French and Italian, Latin and high moral principles, her grandmother was calculating ways and means. Most grammar schools were endowed to offer their somewhat restricted syllabus free of charge, but it cost a lot of money to give a little girl an education fit for a Queen and Arbella unfortunately lacked endowment. Her father had died before she was a year old and Bess, supported by the Queen of Scots, had tried to establish the child's right to inherit his earldom, but without success. The Lennox title and Scottish estates passed to another branch of the Stuart family. Arbella was three when her Lennox grandmother died and the Queen promptly confiscated the Yorkshire estates to pay Lady Lennox's debts. Elizabeth did allow Charles Stuart's widow a modest pension but the jewels which old Lady Lennox had left to her grand-daughter were spirited away into Scotland and never reached Arbella.

Not long after her sixth birthday, tragedy struck again when young Elizabeth Lennox died. 'The poor mother, my wife, takes her daughter's death so grievously and so mourneth and lamenteth that she cannot think of aught but tears', wrote the Earl of Shrewsbury to Francis Walsingham. Bess wept bitterly for the death of her favourite daughter, but characteristically it didn't take her long to consider the financial implications. A week later she was writing to Walsingham herself. 'My assured trust is that her Majesty of her accustomed gracious goodness towards me, will let the same portion it pleased her to bestow on my daughter Lennox and my jewel Arbelle to go to the child for her better education and training up in all good virtue and learning, and so she may the sooner be ready to attend on her Majesty. The child now growing into more years shall stand in more need of more servants and teachers, and I nothing doubt but upon good mediation, her Majesty will think this portion little nought for the child.'

But Queen Elizabeth was not in the habit of regarding any sum of money as 'little nought' and Bess, reckoning up the exorbitant cost of the masters who were to train Arbella up in virtue and learning, returned to the attack on behalf of the 'poor infant' who was wholly dependant on the Queen's 'bounty and goodness'. Elizabeth had allowed £400 a year to young Lady Lennox and £200 to Arbella 'for their better maintenance'. 'I am now, my good Lord', wrote Bess to Lord Burghley, 'to be an humble suitor to the Queen's Majesty that it may please her to confirm that grant of the whole six hundred pounds yearly for the education of my dearest jewel Arbell'. Bess was confident the Queen would agree that to bring up Arbella 'every way as appertaineth and so as she may be able the sooner in service to attend upon her Majesty, will hardly be performed with six hundred pounds yearly in money.'

Before the death of old Lady Lennox, Arbella and her mother had spent some of their time in London but now, as she reminded the Council, Bess was in sole charge of her little grand-daughter. Since she could not be content that the child should be anywhere 'where I may not sometimes see her and daily hear of her well-doing' she was put to the expense of keeping her in house 'with such as are fit to attend upon her and be in her company'. 'For', Bess continued, 'I have an especial care of her standing and condition, not only such as a natural mother hath of her best beloved child, but much greater in respect of how she is in blood to her Majesty: albeit one of the poorest.'

It may not have been entirely tactful to remind the Queen quite so obviously of Arbella's close relationship to her. At any rate, Elizabeth remained unimpressed by the pathetic picture Bess was painting of her poor, orphaned grandchild, and she refused to allow Arbella a penny more than £200 a year. The Queen may well have derived a certain amount of quiet amusement from the fact that the Countess of Shrewsbury's vaunting ambition was leaving her out of pocket.

Bess was far too astute, and too thrifty, to pay for anything if she could persuade someone else to foot the bill, but Arbella's maintenance cannot really have put a very serious strain on the Cavendish and Talbot resources. Certainly, she never went short. Bess was genuinely fond of the child and, besides, she knew a good investment when she saw one.

So the best teachers continued to be engaged and Arbella learnt to dance, to take part in the sports and pastimes proper to her rank and to embroider as skilfully as her grandmother. Nor was her musical education neglected. The Elizabethans were enthusiastic amateur music-makers and anyone with the least pretensions to culture was expected to be able to read music at sight. 'Supper being ended', wrote one gentleman, 'and music books according to the custom being brought to the table, the mistress of the house presented me a part, earnestly requesting me to sing. But when after many excuses, I protested unfeignedly that I could not, everyone began to wonder and some whispered to others demanding how I was brought up.' No one, if Bess had anything to do with it, should be given the chance to make any such disparaging remarks about Arbella's bringing-up.

In the general flowering of the arts which took place during Elizabeth's reign, music held a pre-eminent place. All the Tudors, perhaps it was their Welsh blood, were skilled performers. Henry VIII's talents both as performer and composer, have been well publicised. His daughter played both lute and virginals and encouraged musical talent at her Court. She maintained 'a number of young boys who are required to devote themselves earnestly to the art of singing, and to learn to perform on various sorts of musical instruments, and at the same time to carry on their studies. These boys have their special preceptors in all the various arts, and in particular excellent instructors in music.' Besides the Children of the Chapel Royal, there was no lack of professional musicians to play at Court banquets and festivities and in the public theatres, where, for an hour or more before the play began, the audience could enjoy 'a delightful musical entertainment on organs, lutes and flutes'. Music was an essential part of everyday life enjoyed by all classes: from those whose music came from street singers, the cries of vendors of hot mutton pies, new oysters and lily white mussels, or a fiddler at a village wedding; to the elegant gentleman serenading his lady with the latest air by Dowland or Orlando Gibbons, or a group of courtiers listening to a consort of viols at some great nobleman's house. Arbella certainly took pleasure in her music, and her cousin, the composer Michael Cavendish, was to dedicate a book of songs to her.

Although she spent most of her time in Derbyshire, Arbella did occasionally visit her Cavendish and Talbot relations and her earliest surviving letter is addressed to her grandmother while on one of these trips. 'Good lady grandmother, I have sent your ladyship the ends of my hair, which were cut the sixth day of the moon on Saturday last, and with them a pot of jelly which my servant made. I pray God you find it good. My aunt Cavendish was here on Monday last; she certified me of your ladyship's good health and disposition, which I pray God long to continue. I am in good health. My cousin Mary hath had three little fits of an ague, but she is now well and merry. This with my humble duty unto your ladyship and humble thanks for the letter you sent me last, and craving your daily blessing I humbly cease. Your ladyship's humble and obedient child, Arbella Stewart.'

Bess probably wanted Arbella's hair for some special purpose. Many Elizabethans, from the Queen downwards, took a close interest in astrology and in magic, both black and white. It was the converse side of their nature – the need to propitiate the unseen, dimly understood forces which ruled their lives, the urge to glimpse something of an unknowable, uncertain future. The twelve-year-old Arbella's painstaking letter, with its scraps of family news would have been welcome to her grandmother, but news of far greater importance had reached her in the year 1587 in a letter from her youngest son, Charles Cavendish, when Arbella had been in London staying with Gilbert Talbot and her aunt Mary.

'My lady Arbell hath been once to Court', wrote Charles. 'Her Majesty spake unto her, but not long, and examined her nothing touching her book. She dined in the presence, but my Lord Treasurer bade her to supper; and at dinner, I dining with her and sitting over against him, he asked me whether I came with my niece or no? I said I came with her. Then he spake openly, and directed his speech to Sir Walter Raleigh, greatly in her commendation, as that she had the French, the Italian, played of instruments, danced, wrought needlework, and writ very fair; wished she were fifteen years old, and with that rounded Mr Raleigh in the ear, who answered him it would be a happy thing. At supper he made exceeding much of her; so did he in the afternoon in his great chamber publicly . . . and since he hath asked when she shall come again to Court.'

The meat of Charles Cavendish's letter was contained in the opening sentences. It was natural that Lord Burghley, who had once been William Cecil, a good family man and an old friend of Lady Shrewsbury, should single out her grand-daughter for special attention and kind remarks; what really mattered was that Arbella had 'dined in the presence'. The tables for dinner at Court were laid with tremendous ceremony. The yeomen of the guard, dressed in scarlet with a golden rose on their backs, would bring in a course of twenty-four dishes, served on gilt plate, while twelve trumpets and two kettledrums made the hall ring, but the Queen only dined in public on special occasions, such as Christmas. At other times the maids of honour would lift the meat off the table and carry it into an inner room. Elizabeth took her meals alone 'with very few attendants'. 'It is very seldom that anyone, foreigner or native, is admitted at that time', wrote one observer, 'and then only at the intercession of somebody in power.' But Bess's dearest jewel had been given all the honours. She had received her full due as a princess of the blood and joined the select band who ate with the Queen in private. Nor was this all the recognition Arbella had received. Elizabeth had been overheard to say to the French ambassador's wife: 'Look at her! Look at her well. One day she will be even as I am, and will be a great lady. But I shall have gone before her.'

This was the sort of thing Bess had been waiting to hear. True, the Queen had not named Arbella as her heir in so many words – Elizabeth seldom said anything in so many words – but surely her meaning was plain. All the careful planning, the sleepless nights, the danger and the nervous tension, all the trouble and expense, would be worth it pressed down and running over, if only Bess could live to see her grand-daughter become Queen of England. As she sat reading the news from London that day in 1587, the achieving of her life's ambition seemed a matter of time alone.

4 *The Shrewsbury Scandal*

By the year 1584 the alliance which had once existed
between the Queen of Scots and the Countess of Shrewsbury was at an end and the two ladies were zestfully
engaged in a battle which recognised few of the rules of
war. Bess had accused Mary of having had illicit relations
with her husband – she is even said to have started the
rumour that the Queen of Scots had borne Shrewsbury a
child. Mary retaliated by doing her utmost to ruin Bess.
'I entreat that you will more distinctly show to Queen
Elizabeth the treachery of my honourable hostess, the
Countess of Shrewsbury', she wrote to the French ambassador. 'I had the sure promise of the said Countess', she
went on, 'that if at any time my life were in danger, or if I
were to be removed from here, she would give me the
means of escape, and that she herself could easily elude
danger and punishment in respect to this. She made her
son Charles Cavendish swear to me in her presence that
he would reside in London on purpose to serve me and
warn me of all which passed at the Court, and that he
would actually keep two good strong geldings specially to
let me have speedy intelligence of the death of the Queen,
who was ill at the time, and that he thought to be able to
do this ... The said Countess and her sons used every
possible persuasion to prove to me the danger to which I
was exposed in the hands of the Earl of Shrewsbury, who
would deliver me into the hands of my enemies or allow
me to be surprised by them, in such a manner that,
without the friendship of the said Countess, I was in a very
bad case.' These were only minor examples which Mary
wanted the ambassador to bring to the Queen's attention
(without, of course, disclosing the source of his information), by which Elizabeth could judge what had gone

to make up 'the warp and woof of the intercourse' between Mary and Bess, whom the Queen of Scots could 'place in a terrible position, by giving the names of those persons who, by her express order, have brought me letters in cipher, which she has delivered to me by her own hand'. If Elizabeth decided 'to make skilful enquiry' into Bess's misconduct, Mary 'could disclose other features of greater importance which would cause considerable discomfort to others about her.'

The unfortunate Earl of Shrewsbury, caught in this murderous cross-fire, could only pray to be delivered from two demons – his wife and his prisoner. The Great Shrewsbury Scandal did, in fact, result in Mary being removed from his custody and in a permanent estrangement from Bess, but it was to leave him a broken man, both mentally and physically.

Why did Bess do it? She seldom did anything without a reason, but why had she chosen to stir up trouble on such a dramatic scale? Why had she set out, apparently quite deliberately, to wreck her own marriage? The answers to these questions are not easy to find, but perhaps a closer look at the three people involved and the situation they were trapped in, may provide some clues. By 1584 Mary Queen of Scots had spent fifteen years in the Shrewsburys' care, but she had never become resigned to her loss of liberty and intrigued incessantly with anyone who seemed to offer her the slightest hope of escape. Ever since her flight across the Border, Mary had been the focus of plots by those who favoured her title to the English throne. The Queen of Scots had always been political dynamite, but as the international situation worsened and the cold war with Spain grew hotter, the government became increasingly nervous of attempts to assassinate Elizabeth and put Mary in her place.

The awesome responsibility of guarding Mary was taking its toll of the Earl of Shrewsbury. His position was not made any easier by the constant complaints of his prisoner and constant interference from London. Financially, too, it was a continual drain, especially after Elizabeth decided to economise by cutting down his expense allowance. 'I do not know what account is made of my charges sustained in the keeping of this woman', he wrote to Lord Burghley in July, 1580, 'but assuredly the very charge of victual of my whole household, with the entertainment I do give to my household servants, is not defrayed with the allowance I have had from her Majesty; besides the which I dare be bold to say the wine, the spice, and the fuel that are spent in my house yearly, being valued, come not under £1,000 by the year. Also the loss of plate, the buying of pewter, and all manner of household stuff, which by them is exceedingly spoiled and wilfully wasted, stand me in £1,000 by the year.' The Earl was not including the annuities he had given to his servants, 'to the end to be more faithfully served by them and to prevent any corruption that by want they might be provoked into'; nor the extra money he was spending on the soldiers employed to garrison the household. 'I do leave out an infinite number of hidden charges which I am driven into by keeping this woman', he wrote, '. . . but I do trust that her Majesty, of her own consideration, will so well think of these things that she will not abridge any thing of that which she hath hitherto allowed.'

Elizabeth may have been hoping to force the Queen of Scots into contributing towards her own upkeep, thereby reducing the amount of money she had available to pay her agents and messengers. At any rate, Shrewsbury's protests fell on stony ground. To do him justice, it was not merely the fact that his personal fortune was disappearing at the rate of thirty pounds a day (at least by his own reckoning) which was upsetting him so much. He felt that his honour was at stake. He had never pestered the Queen with unreasonable demands, he reminded Burghley plaintively, nor had he ever complained about the heavy burden his mind had borne and his body had sustained, for he considered himself 'happy and fortunate in living to do her Majesty true and loyal service'. But if his only reward was to be 'by abating the allowance that hitherto I have had, the world must needs think that either my deserts have been very small, or else her Majesty doth make very small account of me'. It was not just the money, the Earl repeatedly assured Lord Burghley. No money could have recompensed him for the loss of liberty, the 'dangering' of his life and the many other discomforts he was exposed to; but 'good my lord', he wrote, '. . . deal so with her Majesty for me as I am not offered so great a disgrace as to abate any part of the allowance'.

Among the many discomforts suffered by the Earl and Countess of Shrewsbury was the disruption of their family life. 'It seems her Majesty has no liking our children should be with us (where this Queen is)', the Earl had complained on another occasion, '. . . which is a great grief unto us. Therefore I pray you, if you shall not think it will be offence to her Majesty, at your good leisure to move her Highness that I may have liberty to go to Chatsworth, to sweeten my house; and that my children may come to me, with her Majesty's favour, when I think good, else they shall not enter within my doors.' The Queen was apparently afraid that too much coming and going by the young Talbots and Cavendishes would provide opportunities for Mary to send and receive uncensored messages. Elizabeth had even objected when Bess's daughter Mary, Gilbert Talbot's wife, came to Sheffield to have her first baby, as it would be 'cause of women and strangers' repair thither', although Shrewsbury assured the Council that only the midwife had been admitted and he himself had christened the child 'to avoid such resort'.

The restrictions imposed on her freedom of movement by the Queen of Scots' constant presence, the perpetual nagging from Elizabeth, her husband's morbid dread of offending the Queen and his nervous preoccupation with his charge would have been irksome to any woman – to one of Bess's independent, energetic temperament they were becoming intolerable. In fact, signs that her fourth marriage was not proving quite so successful as her previous ones had begun to appear as early as the 1570's in a somewhat hectoring letter addressed to the Earl. 'If you cannot get my timber carried', wrote Bess, 'I must be without it, though I greatly want it; but if it would please you to command Hebert, or any other, to move your tenants to bring it, I know they will not deny to do it. I pray you let me know if I shall have the ton of iron. If you cannot spare it, I must make shift to get it elsewhere, for I may not now want it. You promised to send me money afore this time to buy oxen, but I see out of sight out of mind with you.'

Shrewsbury, for his part, was jealous of Bess's Cavendish sons. He also resented her absorption in her building and business interests, and it wasn't long before they were quarrelling bitterly over quite trivial issues. Both husband and wife used Gilbert Talbot, Shrewsbury's eldest surviving son, as a confidant and meeting Gilbert at Bolsover one day, the Earl's conversation soon turned to his marital troubles. According to Gilbert's detailed report to Bess: 'Quoth he, "Gilbert, what talk had my wife with you?" "Marry, my lord," quoth I, "it hath pleased her to talk with me once or twice since my coming; but the matter she most spake of is no small discomfort for me to understand." Then was he very desirous and bade me tell him what. I began: "Truly, sir, with as grieved a mind as ever I saw woman in my life, she told me your lordship was vehemently offended with her, in such sort and with so many words and shows in your anger of evil mind towards her, as thereby your ladyship said you could not but stand doubtful that all his wonted love and affection is clean turned to the contrary, for your ladyship further said you had given him no cause at all to be offended".'

This particular quarrel had arisen over some upholsterers sent by the Earl to Sheffield Lodge and refused admittance by one of Bess's servants, either out of genuine misunderstanding or deliberate malice – the servants in a great household were not above fomenting interesting rows between their employers. Shrewsbury refused to listen to Gilbert's explanations, 'saying it was to no purpose to hear my recital of this matter; for if he listed, he said, he could remember cruel speeches your ladyship used to him, which were such as, quoth he, "I was forced to tell her she scolded like one that came from the Bank" . . . (the Elizabethan equivalent of Billingsgate). So being alighted from his horse all this while, he said, "Let us get up and be going; and I shall have enough to do when I come home".' Gilbert was then obliged to break the news that Bess had departed for Chatsworth in a rage. This was too much for the Earl. ' "What", quoth he, "is she gone from Sheffield? Is her malice such that she will not tarry one night for my coming?" ' Again he refused to listen to Gilbert's attempts to smooth things over, 'saying all the house might discern your ladyship's stomach against him by your departure before his coming. "You know, Gilbert", quoth he, "how often I have cursed the building at Chatsworth for want of her company. You see she careth not for my company, by her going away. I would not have done so to her for five hundred pounds." '

Gilbert Talbot seems to have done his best to make peace between his father and step-mother. He drew such a touching picture of Bess's grief and 'perplexity' at her husband's unkindness, of her conviction that his heart was hardened against her, that all his love and affection had turned to hate and that he preferred her absence to her presence, in spite of her 'dear affection and love to him both in health and sickness', that Shrewsbury began to melt. ' "I know", quoth he, "her love hath been great to me, and mine hath been and is as great to her: for what can a man do more for his wife than I have done and daily do for her?" '

Gilbert told Bess that he believed Shrewsbury wanted a reconciliation, 'if he knew which way to bring it to pass'. But mutual suspicion, jealousy and the effects of continual nervous tension had eaten away the foundations of the marriage and by the early 1580's there was little left but a façade. It was a long time now since the Earl had written tender love letters to Bess.

It was a long time, too, since Bess and the Queen of Scots had sat gossiping together over their needlework. The cooling of this particular friendship seems to date from soon after the birth of Arbella. According to Mary's account, 'nothing has alienated the Countess from me more than the vain hope she has conceived of setting the crown of England on the head of her grand-daughter Arbella'. It is true that once Bess had her own candidate for the succession, Mary and her son became obstacles in the path of her ambition, and Bess had a habit of riding roughshod over obstacles in her path. However, Arbella was eight years old before she took the first practical steps to rid herself of the Queen of Scots.

Some time in the autumn of 1583 she apparently instructed her two younger sons, William and Charles, to start spreading rumours of an illicit relationship between Mary and the Earl of Shrewsbury. There was no love lost between the young Cavendishes and their step-father and no doubt they thoroughly enjoyed the task their mother had set them – they certainly performed it well. Mary's reaction was predictably violent. Through Mauvissière, the French ambassador, she begged that Queen Elizabeth would 'see justice done to me against the Countess of Shrewsbury and her children touching the scandalous reports which they have circulated about me. This is a thing', she went on, 'which I have so much at heart that I shall never have any pleasure until their wickedness is known'.

The rumours naturally grew more and more lurid as they swirled about the Court. Soon it was being openly said that the Queen of Scots had had at least two children by Shrewsbury and Mary wrote furiously to Mauvissière demanding a public vindication of her honour and the 'exemplary punishment' of the scandalmongers. 'I have twice informed you minutely of the scandalous reports which have been circulated of my intimacy with the Earl of Shrewsbury. These have originated with no one but his good lady herself. If the Queen of England does not cause this calumny to be cleared up, I shall be obliged openly to attack the Countess of Shrewsbury herself.'

The Earl clamoured to be allowed to come to Court and clear himself before the Queen of 'the reports and treacheries towards him', but Mary, mewed up at Sheffield, thirsted for revenge. Goaded beyond endurance at her helplessness, the Queen of Scots' rage and frustration presently found expression in her famous 'scandal' letter to Elizabeth, a letter written, so she unblushingly called God to witness, 'without passion and from motives of true sincerity'. In this remarkable document, the Queen of Scots proceeded to inform the Queen of England 'that what the Countess of Shrewsbury has said of you to me is as nearly as possible as follows . . . Firstly, that one to whom she said you had made a promise of marriage before a lady of your chamber, had made love to you an infinite number of times with all the licence and intimacy which can be used between man and wife. But that undoubtedly you were not like other women . . . and you would never lose your liberty to make love and always have your pleasure with new lovers.'

But Bess, it seemed, had not merely accused the Queen of being a raging nymphomaniac. Worse was to follow, in what must surely be one of the most venomous attacks ever made by one woman against another. 'The Countess', wrote Mary, 'in fits of laughter, advised me to place my son among the ranks of your lovers as a thing which would do me good service . . . When I replied that such would be considered an act of mockery, she answered that you were so vain, and had such a good opinion of your beauty – as if you were a goddess from heaven – that she wagered she could easily make you take the matter seriously . . . She said you were so fond of exaggerated adulation, such as the assurance that no one dared to look full into your face since it shone like the sun, that she and other ladies at Court were obliged to make use of similar flattery; that on her last appearance before you, she and the late Countess of Lennox scarcely dared to exchange glances for fear of bursting into laughter at the way in which they were openly mocking you.'

Just what sort of explosion this letter might have provoked had it reached its destination, we shall never know. But either Lord Burghley kept it from the Queen deliberately, or Mary herself thought better of it and never sent it. There is no evidence that Elizabeth ever read it. No doubt it was just as well.

The Queen did, however, take steps to put an end to the Shrewsbury scandal. The Earl came to Court and was officially exonerated before the Council of any undue familiarity with the Queen of Scots. He also had a private interview with Elizabeth. 'His lordship came to her Majesty into her privy chamber. She made him have a stool and to sit down by her, and then talked with him at the least two hours. Amongst other things, my lord took knowledge how he had been slandered by sundry bruits and desired that he might justify himself, saying he would defend his honour and loyalty to her Majesty before all the world. Her Majesty was well pleased with his words, and told him she did account him for a loyal and faithful servant, and esteemed and trusted him as much as any man in England.'

As for Bess, she and her sons now found it prudent to issue official denials. 'Never have they known that the Queen of Scots had had any child since her arrival in this realm, nor had behaved otherwise than a Queen and Princess of her quality should do in honour and chastity', ran the Memorandum of what the Countess of Shrewsbury and her two youngest sons have to declare. Neither, of course, had they ever 'secretly or otherwise reported directly or indirectly anything against the honour of the said Queen of Scots', and held the rumours to be 'very false, scandalous lies, maliciously invented and set on foot'.

All the same, after so much mud-slinging and bitter recriminations, it was obvious that the Queen of Scots would have to be moved and at the beginning of September, 1584 she left Sheffield Castle for the last time.

Again we come back to the question – why did Bess do it? Was she really afraid that her husband had become emotionally, perhaps treasonably, involved with Mary? Or was she just bored with the position of gaoler which had brought no material advantages and was making her as much of a prisoner as the Queen of Scots? A more interesting question is why did Bess use this particular method of getting rid of Mary? The weapon of slander could so easily have proved double-edged. As late as 1584, Elizabeth was trying seriously to come to terms with the Queen of Scots and her son. If a treaty had been concluded and Mary had regained even a limited form of freedom, she would have been a very dangerous enemy indeed. Besides, it was by no means impossible that Mary might yet succeed to the English throne. She was still only forty – ten years younger than her cousin Elizabeth.

As so often in moments of crisis in Bess's life, her motives are either obscure or obscured, but it looks very much as if the Countess, in her usual single-minded fashion, had simply taken the shortest and most certain path towards her objective without too much thought of the consequences. After all, she had taken some pretty considerable risks in the past and got away with them.

One consequence she does not seem to have foreseen, was the final break up of her marriage. This time the Earl of Shrewsbury showed no desire for a reconciliation. 'As to my wife', he wrote to Lord Burghley from Sheffield in 1585, 'she hath sought to impoverish me and to enrich herself. She hath sought the ruin and decay of my house and posterity, to raise up her house and name into that honour. She hath sought my discredit and slander in the face of the world; and albeit she hath a little changed the air, yet she doth carry the old mind, which hath nothing now left to work upon but mine old carcase, whereof I do think she would make a sacrifice if I should receive her again.'

Shrewsbury wanted a separation from Bess, but Queen Elizabeth disapproved of marital disputes among her nobility and ordered the Earl to take his wife back and 'treat her with courtesy'. But the bitterness between them had become too deep, the breach too wide for healing, even by royal command. 'Since that her Majesty hath set down this hard sentence against me', wrote Shrewsbury to the Earl of Leicester, 'to my perpetual infamy and dishonour, to be ruled and overrun by my wife, so bad and wicked a woman, yet her Majesty shall see that I will obey her commandment though no curse or plague in the earth could be so greatly grievous to me.'

Bess, for her part, declared she had 'a great desire for a good and Christian reconciliation' and told the Queen she wanted to live with her husband 'as the bond and knot of matrimony required', but although Shrewsbury had reluctantly agreed to go on supporting her, he flatly refused to be at bed and board with her. He made it quite clear that he had no intention of forgiving and forgetting unless his wife would confess that she had offended him, in writing, on her knees 'and before such as her Majesty shall appoint'.

Bess's proud spirit would never agree to the humiliation of a public apology, but she kept her temper and answered Shrewsbury's accusations of greed with becoming meekness. 'I assure you, my lord,' she wrote, 'my meaning is not to molest or grieve you with demanding, neither I trust it can be thought greediness to demand nothing, for I desire no more than her Majesty's order giveth, and wish your happy days to be many and good . . .'

The Shrewsburys' quarrel was to drag on for another five years – the Earl complaining of his 'wicked and malicious wife' who planned to ruin him in order to benefit her Cavendish progeny – the Countess complaining with equal fluency of her 'strange miseries' and the hard usage of her husband. Rather surprisingly, public sympathy was all with Bess, although the Bishop of Coventry did show some understanding of Shrewsbury's point of view. 'Some will say in your lordship's behalf', he wrote, 'that the Countess is a sharp and bitter shrew, and therefore like enough to shorten your life if she should keep you company. Indeed, my good lord, I have heard some say so, but if shrewdness and sharpness be a just cause of separation between a man and wife, I think few men in England would keep their wives long; for it is a common jest, yet true in some sense, that there is but one shrew in all the world, and every man hath her.'

In spite of many well meant efforts to bring them together, Bess never kept her husband company again. Shrewsbury had had enough – too many demands had been made on him by his wife and his sovereign, and his mind as well as his body began to fail. His last years were spent in the clutches of a mistress who robbed him without compunction, and he died in November 1590, prophesying that by his wife's devices the Lady Arbella Stuart would bring much trouble to his house.

5 *An Insatiable Dream*

The Earl of Shrewsbury's death can only have come as a relief to Bess. She was seventy when she became a widow for the fourth time and there would be no question of any more matrimonial ventures on her own account. Marriage had served her well, in spite of the troubles of the past ten years, but now she meant to steer her own course, alone and unafraid. There was still a lot to be done, and the Dowager Countess looked forward to a busy, exciting future.

Bess was an extremely wealthy woman and now at last she was free to dispose of her fortune as she pleased. It is probably no coincidence, therefore, that barely a month after Shrewsbury's death the new Hardwick Hall began to rise from its foundations.

Today Hardwick stands proud, elegant and graceful, dominating the Derbyshire landscape just as it did on a day in October nearly four hundred years ago when Bess first saw it completed – a statement in glass and stone of her own individual genius, and the latest of a string of houses she had been building and re-building for more than forty years. Hardwick Hall is the only one of those houses to survive, but it is the one which most completely expresses the personality of the yeoman's daughter who had risen in the world by her own efforts, her own shrewdness, courage and determination.

It has been said that Bess intended Hardwick to be a showcase for Arbella Stuart, who, if all went well, might one day become Queen of England. Bess's enemies never hesitated to accuse her of insatiable ambition, but was her most splendid achievement merely another status symbol? Was it, perhaps, all part of a subconscious need to go on proving herself? Or was her building fever the outlet for a creative impulse which would not be denied? Bess may simply have been thinking of her own sons. Chatsworth, which had been the centre of the bitterest disputes with Shrewsbury, was intended for Henry Cavendish, but there were also William and Charles to be considered. Whatever it was that drove her on to build more and yet more houses, she was certainly not alone.

'There was never the like number of fair and stately houses as have been built and set up from the ground since her Majesty's reign', remarked Francis Bacon; 'insomuch that there have been reckoned in one shire that is not great, to the number of thirty-three which have been all new-built within that time – whereof the meanest was never built for two thousand pounds.' All over the country, in fact, 'fair and stately' houses were rising to proclaim the accumulated wealth and self-confidence of the Tudor age.

William Harrison, who has left us such a vivid picture of England in the second half of the sixteenth century, wrote that: 'Such manors and houses of our gentlemen as be lately builded are commonly either of brick or hard stone, or both, their rooms large and comely, and houses of office further distant from their lodgings. Those of the nobility are likewise wrought with brick and hard stone, as provision may best be made, but so magnificent and stately as the basest house of a baron doth often match in our days with some honours of princes in old time.' The fact that there was more money about, was not the only reason for this new luxuriance in domestic architecture. The Elizabethan man of property no longer needed to anticipate unfriendly visits from his neighbours. He no longer needed to encumber himself with moats and bastions and other such defensive outworks. True, Hardwick has its turrets, six of them, silhouetted dramatically against the skyline, but Bess's turrets were not intended as vantage points for marksmen. They added height, grace and symmetry to the building. They were decorated with coronets and strapwork and, catching the eye from every angle, the initials E.S. Elizabeth Shrewsbury was justly pleased with her handiwork. She saw no reason to conceal the fact, and high above the front door her coat of arms flaunted pride of ownership, pride of achievement before an admiring or an envious world.

The most startling feature of Hardwick, though, is the lavish use of glass – another sign of a new outlook, literally, on life. 'Of old time', commented William Harrison, 'our country houses, instead of glass, did use much lattice, and that made either of wicker or fine rifts of oak in checkerwise. I read also that some of the better sort did make panels of horn instead of glass. But as horn in windows is now quite laid down in every place, so lattices are also grown into less use, because glass is come to be so plentiful. Only the clearest glass is most esteemed and each one that may will have it for his building.'

In spite of some disparaging remarks about 'Hardwick Hall more glass than wall', Bess was determined that her new house should be 'lightsome' and during the building operations she insisted in 'highing' the great windows still further. Her influence is everywhere apparent, pervading Hardwick like a physical presence. She knew how to use grandeur to make a deliberate effect. She also knew how to make a home. Compared with the magnificent facade, the low, pillared entrance is inviting, almost cosy in its welcome. Bess would have agreed, at least in part, with Francis Bacon's dictum that: 'Houses are built to live in, and not to be looked upon; therefore let use be preferred before uniformity, except where both may be had. Leave the goodly fabrics of houses, for beauty only, to the enchanted palaces of the poets, who build them with small cost.'

Hardwick took seven years to complete and was certainly not built at small cost; though, as always, Bess kept a sharp eye on the accounts and on November 14th 1591 decided to change her clerk of works. 'Memorandum', she wrote, 'Sir Harry Jenkinson to take charge of the workmen and keeping of the book.' She also kept a sharp eye on the progress of the work and tolerated no slackness or scamping. 'Because the walls rise and be not well nor all of one colour, the most to be whited at the plasterers' charge.'

There is no mention of an architect in Bess's account books, though the 'platt' for Hardwick was probably drawn by Robert Smythson who had designed nearby Wollaton Hall. But any professional architect's plans were subject to constant revision and alteration by Bess herself. During the time the new Hardwick was going up, she was living within sight of the work at Hardwick Old Hall. The Old Hall is now a ruin, but Bess had enlarged and rebuilt her birthplace, wishing, so it was said, 'to keep her cradle beside her bed of state'.

Materials for the new building were drawn from her own resources. Timber came from her broad estates, lead from the mines bequeathed by her first husband, the long dead Robert Barlow. Alabaster was brought from Tutbury, which had once housed Mary Queen of Scots, blackstone from Ashford near Bakewell. Skegby and Crich supplied lime, Wingfield the famous glass.

William Harrison would certainly have approved of this sensible policy. 'Our elders have from time to time', he wrote, 'following our natural vice in misliking of our own commodities at home and desiring those of other countries abroad, most esteemed the Caen stone that is brought hither from Normandy; and many even in these days, do covet in their works almost to use none other ... Howbeit, experience on the one side and our skilful masons on the other, do affirm that we have quarries enough and good enough in England sufficient for us to build withal, if the peevish contempt of our own commodities, and delectations to enrich other countries did not catch such foolish hold upon us.'

Bess had far too much commonsense to put her money unnecessarily into other people's pockets. Hardwick is built of sandstone cut from the quarry in the cliff below the Old Hall and carried up to the site of the new building on pack horses by Robert Holm and his labourer. The contract for the stonework was let to master mason John Roads and his brother Christopher. 'Paid to John Roads for hewing of two windows containing in measure sixty-four foot apiece for the turrets, forty-eight shillings.' The accounts continue: 'Paid Roads for hewing ninety-eight foot of window stuff for the highing of eight windows for two of the turrets upon the leads, three pounds, fifteen shillings ... Paid John Roads for setting two hundred and eighteen foot of architrave, frieze and cornice for the two turrets at threepence the foot and so he is paid for setting of all the turrets.'

As well as using local materials, Bess employed local craftsmen whenever she could. The most famous of these was Abraham Smith, the plasterer. Thirty years earlier Bess had written to Sir John Thynne, begging for the loan of the plasterer who was 'flowering' the hall at Longleat. Then she discovered Abraham, who came from nearby Ashford, and no longer needed to ask for outside help. The use of plaster for interior decoration was a fairly recent innovation and the work was complicated and highly skilled. According to Harrison: 'In plastering of our fairest houses over our heads, we use to lay first a line or two of white mortar, tempered with hair, upon laths which are nailed one by another – sometimes upon reeds of wickers, more dangerous for fire – and finally cover all with the aforesaid plaster, which, beside the delectable whiteness of the stuff itself, is laid on so even and smoothly as nothing in my judgement can be done with more exactness.'

Abraham Smith was more than just another skilled workman. He was an artist in his own right, and as such was a highly valued employee, paid by the quarter by Bess herself. One quarter's wages amounted to £3 . 6 . 8d. and in September, 1592, he received a present of forty shillings 'against his wedding'. Abraham more than repaid this generosity by the exquisite quality of his work at Hardwick. He was equally at home as a mason and carpenter but it was in decorative plasterwork that he excelled. He was responsible for the famous frieze in the High Presence Chamber, for the moulded ceilings, the goddess Ceres in the Paved Room and the intricate strap-work designs over the hall chimneypiece. The great coat of arms in the hall is also his work.

There were some spoilsports who disapproved of this kind of display. 'Everyone vaunts himself', complained John Stubbes, 'crying with open mouth, "I am gentleman, I am worshipful, I am honourable, I am noble" and I cannot tell what. "My father was this, my father was that. I am come of this house, I am come of that . . ." ' The Countess of Shrewsbury would have paid no attention to such pusillanimous nonsense. Whatever her faults, Bess was not afflicted by false modesty and, anyway, for one of her dynastic ambitions the full – sometimes rather over-optimistic – representation of armorial bearings was a matter of important practical significance.

Wherever Bess went in Hardwick Hall she was able to enjoy the fruits of her own planning and her own ingenuity. The staircase, for instance, does not, as one would expect, spring directly from the entrance hall. Instead, it is tucked away, almost secretively, leading upwards with a mysterious, seductive promise of further delights in store. Some people, such as Francis Bacon, had definite ideas on how a staircase should be constructed. 'Let the stairs to the upper rooms be upon a fair open newel – a pillar of stone or wood, where the steps terminate in a winding staircase – and finely railed in with images of wood, cast into a brass colour; and a very fair landing place at the top. But this to be if you do not appoint any of the lower rooms for a dining place of servants. For otherwise you shall have the servants' dinner after your own: for the steam of it will come up as in a tunnel.'

The thought of stale smells of cabbage wafting up the stairs at Hardwick is a vulgarity not to be contemplated. Neither is there any heavy, elaborately carved balustrade. Bess's staircase is simple to the point of starkness. The treads are of stone instead of the more usual timber and made very wide and shallow. Was this perhaps her sole concession to encroaching age? On the half-landing there is a place to pause and rest, a place, too, to be quiet in, to have a private conversation before reaching the Long Gallery. The Gallery is 170 feet long – a place for taking exercise when the weather was bad, a place for entertaining, for gossiping or plotting in the window embrasures. The Long Gallery was a feature of all Elizabethan mansions, but typically enough none were as splendid as the Gallery at Hardwick.

Here Thomas Acres, the marble mason, demonstrated his art on the elaborately carved chimneypieces. Acres was another master craftsman. Like Abraham Smith he was paid by the quarter and had two apprentices, Lawrence Dolphin and Miles Padly, working under him. His was an exacting trade and his name appears frequently in the building accounts for 1596. 'Paid to Thomas Acres for his charge to Tutbury, twenty-one pence, and for shoeing his horse, threepence. His charges and his man's at Ashford, three shillings and fourpence for choosing of blackstone . . . Two stone of chalk for Thomas Acres to polish blackstone . . . Two pounds of rosin for Acres, fourpence. Half a pound of wax, sixpence. For leather to polish blackstone with, fourpence and for a file to whet the blackstone saw, fourpence . . . Given the 10th of May unto Acres' wife in respect of her husband's device of sawing of blackstone to buy her a gown withal, forty shillings.'

John Painter's wife also received twenty shillings to compensate her when she was robbed. Thoughtful gestures like these naturally endeared Bess to her workpeople. Although she was a hard mistress, demanding the highest standards, she was always ready to reward and appreciate good service.

The ceiling and cornice in the Long Gallery were entrusted to another plasterer, John Marker, and the frieze was painted by John Painter – a name which may have been a convenient substitute for something unpronounceably foreign. Painter occupied an important position, acting as a sort of general foreman as well as exercising his own craft, for which he had to be provided with a lot of special material. For example, four gallons of linseed oil at fourpence the gallon and a runlet to put the oil in. Two pounds of yellow ochre cost another fourpence and two hundredths of painting gold came to twelve shillings. He also needed a pound of red lead and six pounds of varnish which was bought at Nottingham at sixteen pence the pound, not to mention two pounds of verdigrease which cost six shillings and eightpence. Other exotic sounding commodities ordered by John Painter include fernando bark, brasill, blockwood, allorme, fusticke and coppris, but his list ends with a prosaic request for a pound of gum and two pounds of glue costing one and fivepence.

So the work went on all through the 1590's, and a small army of masons, paviours and wallers, carpenters, joiners, sawyers, slaters and smiths, painters, plumbers and glaziers laboured to make Bess's dreams a reality. No detail of expenditure was too small to be recorded in her account books – half a thousand of twopenny nails for Abraham Smith, eightpence paid for making a cradle for the glazier, sevenpence for one horseload of lime, even a penny for mending pack saddles. The average wages of skilled men seem to have varied from between fourpence and sixpence a day, and again their names have been faithfully recorded. There was William Bromley, the carpenter, and his son Henry, another carpenter. Henry Neall, mason; John Ward, Thomas Beane, Thomas Durham, and William Plumber who brought up the water. There was Robert Cordley, who made the little lime kiln as big as the great and was paid two shillings for his labour. There were Walter Chellten and John Batley, Edward Worthington the slater, Richard Mallery and Gilbert Moore and a host of other homely, forgotten Englishmen, whose immortality lies in the beauty they made with their hands.

When Bess and Arbella moved across from the Old Hall in 1597 some work was still going on, but Bess could congratulate herself on having created a setting fit for a future Queen. In planning Hardwick, Bess had retained some at least of the features she had known in the country houses of her youth. The Great Hall had once been the core of the great house, used for eating, living and entertaining – used by the whole household. But as 'The Family' gradually began to withdraw into separate quarters, the Great Hall began to decline. Bess was too much of a conservative to dispense with the Hall entirely, even though it was no longer used for its original purpose and became more of a place where visitors were greeted and servants lounged and gossiped and played cards. She also kept the minstrels' gallery and built it to act as a bridge, running across the Hall from one side of the house to the other.

Hardwick was too far from London to make it a resort of important visitors in the normal course of events, but the great house was the natural centre of local society, where the Dowager Countess could entertain her neighbours and those of her relatives with whom she was still on speaking terms. After Shrewsbury's death Bess had inevitably quarrelled with the new Earl, her old ally Gilbert Talbot and Gilbert's wife, her daughter Mary.

Bess of Hardwick
as Lady Cavendish

2. Sir William Cavendish

Arbella Stuart at two years old

4. Bess of Hardwick,
Countess of Shrewsbury

George Talbot,
Earl of Shrewsbury

7. Mary Queen of Scots
during her captivity

Queen Elizabeth

8. Hardwick Hall: the West Front showing the pill

main entrance with Bess's arms and initials on the skyline

9. *Above:* the Entrance Hall at Hardwick showing the Minstrels' Gallery

10. *Left:* the main staircase at Hardwick

11. *Top right:* the Presence or High Great Chamber at Hardwick

12. *Bottom right:* the Long Gallery

13. The State Bedroom at Hardwick

14. The mysterious 'Scots' Room at Hardwick

Her youngest son, Charles, sided with the Talbots in this dispute and had fallen into similar disfavour. But William Cavendish, always his mother's favourite, spent a lot of time at Hardwick with his wife and family, and Bess remained on good terms with her eldest daughter Frances and her family.

The Long Gallery was ideal for dancing, and it is not difficult to imagine Bess watching indulgently while her friends and the younger members of her family enjoyed themselves. Her thoughts would be far away, planning future triumphs, thinking of a day when a group of tired, mud-spattered men would ride their spent horses across the courtyard – of a day when Arbella, with Bess at her side, would stand in the Long Gallery waiting to receive the messengers who had come to tell her that Queen Elizabeth had named her to succeed to the English throne. Then Hardwick would indeed be a scene of brilliance and of splendour. The house, anchored like a great ship to the crest of the ridge, would blaze with light from end to end – the halls and galleries and chambers would be alive with stir and bustle and music. No distance would then be too far for the world to travel to pay its court to Bess of Hardwick's grand-daughter.

6 Cousin to King James

Ever since the day of her birth in the autumn of 1575, Arbella Stuart had been the central pivot round which Bess of Hardwick's life revolved – the object of her love and care – the focus of her dynastic ambitions. In spite of all her other pre-occupations, Bess had lavished time, energy and money on the task of preparing her grand-daughter for a great future. Now, as Arbella grew into womanhood, she was becoming important to certain other members of her family.

King James of Scotland had a special reason for taking an interest in young Arbella Stuart. She was not merely his cousin, she was also his closest rival for the position of Queen Elizabeth's heir presumptive. As long as the Queen continued to refuse to name her successor, James could not be quite easy in his mind about the future and in December, 1591, he apparently decided it would be a good idea if he and Arbella got to know each other. 'Although the natural bonds of blood, my dear cousin,' he wrote, 'be sufficient for the good entertainment of amity, yet will I not abstain from those common offices of letters.' James could no longer forbear to signify to Arbella the content-ment he had received by hearing of her 'so virtuous be-haviour', wherein he prayed her most heartily to continue. 'Not that I doubt thereof', he went on hastily, 'being certified of so full concourse of nature and nurriture, but that you may be the more encouraged to proceed in your virtuous demeanour, reaping the fruit of so honest esti-mation, the increase of your honour and joy, and your kindly affected friends, especially of me, whom it pleaseth most to see so virtuous and honourable scions arise of that race whereof we have both our descent. Now, hearing more certain notice of the place of your abode, I will the more frequently visit you by my letters, which I mean to be glad to do in person, expecting also to know from time to time of your estate by your own hand, which I look you will not weary to do, being first summoned by me, knowing how far I shall be pleased thereby.' But after this somewhat laborious attempt at cousinly amiability the correspondence lapsed – at least there is no record that Arbella ever replied.

James was now in his mid-twenties and already married to Anne of Denmark. Why had he not taken Arbella as his wife? Her claim would then have been merged in his – her competition removed. As for Arbella, her future would have been assured, and although James might leave a good deal to be desired as a husband, she would have been spared much other unhappiness. The idea had been suggested. When Arbella was ten years old, an envoy had been sent up to Scotland by Francis Walsingham with instructions 'to deal particularly with the King about his marriage, and to recommend the King of Denmark's daughter to him or the Lady Arbella Stuart'. According to Mary Queen of Scots, Bess had also at one time hoped to match Arbella with James. But the plan came to nothing. Perhaps Queen Elizabeth had vetoed it: James and Arbella together might have become rather too powerful a partnership. James himself does not seem to have shown any enthusiasm, and finally settled on the Danish princess for reasons probably not unconnected with the size of her dowry. But he continued to take an anxious interest in Arbella's future. He was nagged by the fear that Elizabeth might decide on a foreign alliance for her, and the last thing James wanted to see was his cousin married to some powerful prince who would be in a position to enforce her claim. To try and prevent such a disaster, he put forward his kinsman Ludovic Stuart, on whom had devolved the dukedom (previously the earldom) of Lennox which had once belonged to Arbella's father. 'When I came hither first', reported Thomas Fowler to Lord Burghley from Scotland in 1589, 'all the King's care was how he might procure the Lady Arbella for wife to the said Duke, and would have sent to the Queen's majesty therein; but asking my opinion I discouraged him. Then he thought to desire in general terms to have the bestowing of her. I answered that yet he was liker to succeed by dealing in special, for no doubt her Majesty would know how she should be bestowed.'

James was by no means the only person interested in the question of how Arbella should be bestowed. As long as the English succession remained in doubt, her prospects would be discussed by statesmen in the capitals of Europe – whispered over in discreet Flemish taverns where Walsingham's agents and their informants gathered. In Paris and Munich, Brussels and Madrid, everyone was eager to know 'what reputation' the Lady Arbella was in – who was the latest candidate for her hand. Lord Burghley was informed that 'the Duke of Lennox keeps an especial person in England to follow his causes there, and that still, by the advice of great personages here (Scotland), he longs after Arbella'.

In the reports which flowed in from English spies and undercover agents abroad during the last two decades of the century, Arbella's name keeps cropping up. 'I beseech you send me word whether you be not made acquainted with matters that one Barnes hath in handling, touching the Lady Arbella. I pray you send me her picture, for that there is some one very desirous to see it...' 'The Earl of Westmorland says that Barnes is treating a marriage between Lady Arbella and the Duke of Parma's son.' A spy in the household of the Adelantado of Castile, 'who on other occasions has given true reports', was asked 'what he had heard about the marriage of Arbella with the prince of Condè. He replied that although it was spoken of at first, he had heard no more about it...' In 1592 Reinold Boseley reported that 'Sir Edward Stafford's servant is employed from beyond sea to practise with Arbella about a marriage between her and the Duke of Parma's son. He was sent once before for her picture, and has been thrice in England this year . . .' According to 'J.B.' in Brussels, 'An English priest writing from Rome says that the Spanish ambassador has heard from France that the Queen will give Arbella in marriage to the French King and declare him her successor . . .' A month later 'J.B.' was writing again: 'The news that I told you before, sent in cipher in great secrecy, is now in the Roman Gazetteer, viz. that the marriage treaty between the French King and the great Duke (of Tuscany) cools, for the Queen of England has promised him a near cousin of her own, whom she loves much and whom she intends to make her heir and successor.' But the Venetian ambassador in Germany heard a different story. 'They say the Queen is very jealous of the prosperity of the French, her ancient rebels and foes', he told the Doge. 'Some weeks ago she told the Scottish ambassador that his most Christian Majesty had demanded in marriage Arbella, daughter of Charles Stuart . . . who is a pretender to the Crown no less than the King of Scotland. The Scottish ambassador complained to the French ambassador, who pointed out the improbability of this, as his Majesty had concluded a contract of marriage with Tuscany.' Elsewhere it was being said that Robert Cecil, old Lord Burghley's son 'intends to be king by marrying Arbella and now lacks only the name'. Others heard of a plan to marry her to the Earl of Hertford's younger son, and there was a 'report of a marriage between Duke Matthias (son of the Emperor Maximilian) and the Lady Arbella'.

But while the rumours multiplied and the gossip spread, other plans were being laid for Arbella. In July, 1597, Thomas North, one of the Earl of Essex's foreign correspondents, wrote from Munich '. . . This doctor Turner and the Spanish legate have had conference with me touching Mistress Arbella, how beautiful, how virtuous and how inclined; yea, they seem how some plot may be laid for her conveyance out of England. Therein I answered fitting their humours.'

This was not the first time such information had reached England. The English Catholics in exile and the missionary priests – shock troops trained at the seminaries at Douai and Rome, who willingly risked a horrible death to win their fellow countrymen back to the Faith – saw in Arbella, a young woman, unmarried and still malleable, a potentially useful tool in their campaign to restore the Catholic religion in England. Early in the 1590's the confession of a captured Jesuit priest indicated the existence of a plot to convey Arbella 'by stealth out of England into Flanders, which, if it be done, I promise you she shall shortly after visit Spain'. This particular ploy seems to have been connected with an ambitious scheme by Sir William Stanley, a prominent figure among the English exiles, to kill the Queen and 'enter the realm with a number of men'. It was apparently hoped that 'the Queen being thus suddenly taken away, all in England would fall together by the ears, and extreme confusion ensue; and that Sir William Stanley's party would be able to prevail'.

The Council took the matter seriously enough to send a warning to Bess and she responded with characteristic vigour. 'My good Lord', she wrote to Burghley, 'I was at the first much troubled to think that so wicked and mischievous practises should be devised to entrap my poor Arbell and me, but I put my trust in the Almighty, and will use such diligent care as I doubt not but to prevent whatsoever shall be attempted by any wicked persons against the poor child . . . I will not have any unknown or suspected person to come to my house. Upon the least suspicion that may happen here, any way, I shall give advertisement to your lordship. I have little resort to me;

my house is furnished with sufficient company. Arbell walks not late; at such time as she shall take the air, it shall be near the house and well attended on. She goeth not to anybody's house at all. I see her almost every hour in the day. She lieth in my bedchamber. If I can be more precise than I have been, I will be. I am bound in nature to be careful for Arbell. I find her loving and dutiful to me, yet her own good and safety is not dearer to me, nor more by me regarded, than to accomplish her Majesty's pleasure and that which I think may be for her service. I would rather wish many deaths than to see this or any such like wicked attempt to prevail.'

Bess assured Lord Burghley that she was keeping a sharp look out for 'seminaries' or similarly suspicious characters, and would not allow 'such traitorous and naughty persons' to be harboured near any of her houses, for they were 'the likest instruments to put a bad matter in execution'. She had had some doubts about 'one Morley who hath attended on Arbell and read to her for the space of three years and a half'. Morley had apparently claimed that Arbella had promised him an annuity and been unwise enough to show himself 'to be much discontented' when this did not materialise. Bess was not standing for that, 'and withal having some cause to be doubtful of his forwardness in religion, took occasion to part with him. After he was gone from my house', she went on, 'and all his stuff carried from hence, the next day he returned again, very importunate to serve without standing upon any recompense, which made me more suspicious and the more willing to part with him.' 'I will have those that shall be sufficient in learning, honest and well-disposed, so near as I can', wrote her ladyship firmly.

The danger that Arbella might be spirited away and used as a figurehead by one of the factions, native and foreign, now beginning to jockey for power as the Elizabethan era drew towards its close was no illusion. There were a number of Catholic families among Bess's neighbours where a determined group of conspirators could have found shelter, and certain members of her own clan were not entirely above suspicion. Two women, one in her late seventies, the other barely out of her teens, living alone in a remote country district might have looked easy prey to some people (at least to those not personally acquainted with the Dowager Countess of Shrewsbury), but Bess was to prove more than a match for any would-be kidnappers. From now on the unfortunate Arbella, guarded day and night, became little more than her grandmother's prisoner.

Far away in London the uncertain future continued to be discussed above her head. Everyone had their own ideas, their own hopes and fears. John Harington, Elizabeth's 'saucy godson', writing in the year after Essex's execution, tells us something of what the atmosphere was like at Court. 'My Lady Arbella also now began to be spoken of and much commended, as she is well worthy for many noble parts, and the Earl of Essex in some glancing speeches gave occasion to have both himself and her honourable friends to be suspected of that which I suppose was no part of their meaning. But . . . the policy of the State thinking it time to have a heavier counterpoise against the King of Scots, a competitor grown now so famous over Europe for wisdom . . . the Infanta of Spain was entertained with many kind messages, goodly jewels and tokens, rebatoes and ruffes and such pretty puppets.' But now, wrote Harington, this Spanish conceit was 'grown out of request' and 'all is suddenly turned French'. So much so that 'some wise and honest men fear there is some strange matter in working . . . I pray God all turn to the best', sighed honest John Harington, 'but I like it not.' As every good Englishman knew, 'the kindness and courtesy of France is often dangerous but ever costly to England'.

The Spanish Infanta, daughter of Philip II, who could

trace her descent from John of Gaunt, was naturally the favourite candidate of the Spanish bloc and their allies; although others of varying degrees of implausibility were suggested in a report prepared for the King of Spain based on 'information' and advice from the English Jesuit Father Persons. 'As your Majesty will not take the country for yourself', ran Person's report, 'they (the English Catholics) propose in the first place, for the succession, the Infanta Isabel; in the second, the Duke of Savoy, who being a widower might marry Arbella Stuart, who is a Catholic and has many friends; in the third place, the Duke of Parma or his son; in the fourth place, the son of the Earl of Worcester, an English Catholic of good parts, who, although he has no claim to the Crown, might marry the daughter of the Earl of Derby.'

But while the Spanish Council of State solemnly deliberated; while James fretted in his bleak northern capital; while Arbella paced the walks at Hardwick and Bess waited impatiently for news, the oracle herself remained inscrutable. The ageing Queen Elizabeth was still in excellent health and had no intention of putting either James or Bess out of their misery. Arbella was a useful pawn in the political game at chess. She could be dangled before this or that foreign prince as occasion demanded. If James showed signs of getting out of hand, the Queen could always suddenly discover a marked preference for her young kinswoman in Derbyshire. It suited her, though, to keep Arbella at Hardwick, where she would have little opportunity to make a party for herself and where, of course, Bess had to bear the expense and responsibility of keeping her safe.

The months dragged by and Bess began to wonder if the hard work, good money and careful planning she had invested in her grand-daughter were going to be wasted after all.

No opportunity was missed of propitiating the Queen

with dutiful letters and expensive gifts and in January, 1600 one of Elizabeth's ladies wrote to the young Countess of Shrewsbury: 'I have . . . presented your ladyship's New Year's gift, together with my Lady Arbella's, to the Queen's majesty, who hath very graciously accepted thereof, and taken an especial liking to my Lady Arbella's.' In spite of her quarrel with Bess, Mary Talbot kept a watching brief on Arbella's interests at Court and her informant's letter continued, 'Whereas in former letters of your ladyship's, your desire was that her Majesty would have that respect of my Lady Arbella that she might be carefully bestowed to her Majesty's good liking . . . her Majesty told me that she would be careful of her, and withal returned a token to my Lady Arbella, which is not so good as I could wish it, nor so good as her ladyship deserveth.'

This was cold comfort. Arbella had now passed her twenty-first birthday and she was not even betrothed. Then, in March, 1602, the horizon brightened briefly. A French alliance was being actively discussed and a French Duke was to pay a State visit to London. 'The arrival of the Duke of Nevers is daily expected,' wrote a Jesuit priest to Father Persons. 'The Earl of Northumberland is appointed to meet him. Many of the most rich hangings are fetched out of the Tower to adorn the Court and great preparations made for his honourable entertainment. The general opinion is that he cometh out of curiosity to see the Court and country, but in special I hear he desireth secretly a sight of the Lady Arbella, for that some great person here, bearing the French in hand [tells him], that it shall be in his power to dispose of the succession after her Majesty's death, by preferring whom he please to match with the said lady. This duke, albeit a married man, being a great favourite, is fed in hope thereof for himself – if his wife die – or some friend, and thereupon under colour of some other embassy undertaketh this voyage.

How probable this may be, I leave to your consideration ... Only this much I can assure you, that the Lady Arbella is shortly to come to London.'

The Duke of Nevers came to London and was suitably entertained. The Lady Arbella stayed at Hardwick, not allowed to speak to anyone but a carefully chosen group of attendants and her grandmother's friends. The Queen continued to ignore her existence. In Catholic circles abroad her prestige slumped as word got round that my Lady Arbella was a notable Puritan. All the same, in 1602, the Lady Arbella was still being regarded by some people as a feasible alternative to James. She had the advantage of being native born – the English prejudice against 'strangers' was notorious – and there were those who would have rallied to her support, given the right kind of encouragement. But secluded in Derbyshire, she had no popular following. It is probably no exaggeration to say that the great majority of the English people did not even know of her existence and, as John Harington remarked, 'we are not like to be governed by a lady shut up in a chamber from all her subjects and most of her servants, and seen but on holy days'. Arbella suffered from a worse disadvantage than this. She had inherited none of her grandmother's robust commonsense, none of Bess's opportunism – that unerring instinct for when to act, when to take a risk, when to remain meek and passive. Arbella, to her sorrow, was all Stuart with all the fatal Stuart capacity for self-delusion. Her visit to Court in 1587 is said to have ended in disgrace. According to a story picked up by the Venetian ambassador, she had 'displayed such haughtiness that she soon began to claim the first place; and one day on going into chapel she herself took precedence of all the princesses who were in her Majesty's suite; nor would she retire though repeatedly told to do so by the Master of the ceremonies, for she said that by God's will that was the very lowest place that could possibly be given her. At this the Queen in indignation, ordered her back to her private life without so much as seeing her before she took her leave, or indeed ever afterwards.' This item of gossip, related many years after the event, may well be exaggerated and inaccurate in details but it has an underlying ring of truth. It would have been natural enough if a child of eleven had let the excitement of the occasion go to her head – but it was a mistake that a child in Arbella Stuart's position could not afford to make; a mistake that Bess of Hardwick would not have made, even at that age, and nor would Elizabeth Tudor.

7 *This Costly Countess*

By the end of the 1590's Bess of Hardwick, now approaching her eightieth birthday, was comfortably settled in her splendid new house with her grand-daughter Arbella, her son William Cavendish, William's wife and children, and a staff of between sixty and seventy servants. This was housekeeping on a grand scale, and even when the family dined alone formal ceremony was punctiliously observed.

There were two meals a day at Hardwick; one at eleven in the morning, the other at five o'clock in the afternoon, but the ritual of laying the table and serving the food – a scaled down version of the ceremony observed at Court – started a full hour beforehand. It involved the Yeomen of the Ewer, Pantry, Buttery and Cellar, the Gentleman Carver, the Sewer and several waiters, all under the supervision of the Gentleman Usher.

Ceremonial played an important part in Elizabethan life and there were sound practical reasons for much of this apparently time-wasting procedure. For one thing, the habit of employing large numbers of 'gentlemen' servants – often poor relations of the noble families they served, or the penniless younger sons of small landowners and squires – gave a home, a regular occupation and a start in life to a restless, ambitious section of the population which might otherwise have got into various kinds of dangerous mischief. The exaggerated deference paid to the heads of great households also helped to bolster authority in an age when the enforcement of law and order lay almost entirely in the hands of the magistrates – themselves masters of households. 'In pompous ceremonies a secret of government doth much consist', wrote a far-seeing contemporary, and the Elizabethan establishment, from the Queen downwards, fully exploited this simple axiom.

Under the eye of its formidable mistress, the complicated machinery of Hardwick Hall ran on oiled wheels, but for Arbella Stuart the atmosphere of effortless luxury which surrounded her can only have served to emphasise the sterility of her life. Apart from occasional visits to relations, Arbella had spent all her life in Derbyshire, waiting for a sign from the Queen that she intended to recognise her as heir to the throne; or even that Elizabeth would arrange a suitable marriage for her young cousin. Time had passed and no sign had come. Arbella, now in her late twenties, remained with her grandmother, still being treated like a child, financially dependent on Bess and watched day and night in case she became the focus of some plot against the Crown.

Studious by nature, Arbella sought solace in her books, her 'dead counsellors' as she called them. She passed some of the endless, empty days by learning Greek and Hebrew and reading with the Reverend John Starkey, tutor to her Uncle William's sons. But she was a high-spirited girl, brought up to believe in the greatness of her destiny and not surprisingly she was finding life at Hardwick more and more intolerable. She told John Starkey that 'she thought of all the means she could to get from home, by reason she was hardly used in despiteful and disgraceful words ... which she could not endure; and this seemed not feigned'. Starkey was to declare, 'for oftentimes, being at her book, she would break forth into tears'. Starkey, moved by Arbella's distress, 'promised that, if it would please her to use my service, I would deliver her letters or messages while I stayed in town'. The tutor was also anxious to escape from Hardwick. He had been with the Cavendishes for ten years 'in servitude and homage', as he put it, in expectation of a living which William continued to withhold. All the same, Starkey was very reluctant to risk offending the family and seems to have regretted his impulsive offer of help. But Arbella promised that in return she would employ him as her chaplain 'if she were appointed to another place', and when Starkey left for London in the summer of 1602, he had agreed to do some errands for her. Before his departure, Arbella told him that Bess had threatened to take away what money and jewels she had, 'but she had prevented her by sending them away into Yorkshire'. She also hinted that 'she had good friends and more than all the world knew of'.

While Arbella and Starkey were making their arrangements over the study table, the daily round at Hardwick continued its accustomed pattern about them. Servants in an Elizabethan household played an intrinsic part in their employers' lives, acting as friends and confidants, companions and entertainers, but they themselves were organised according to a strict hierarchy. The Steward headed the list. He was his master's agent and right-hand man in the management of the household and estate, and occupied a position of considerable power and influence. The Steward had 'to see what demesnes of his lord is most meet to be taken into his hands so well for meadow, pasture, as arable, and those to be employed to his lord's best profit. He is also to make choice of such bailiffs of husbandry for his lord's profit as shall be able to buy and sell with good discretion ... He is to receive all sums of money of the Receiver General for the making of all provisions, so well ordinary as extraordinary, and for reparations, to pay bills of allowances and servants' wages ... Besides, his hand is warrant to the Receiver for what sums soever for his lord's affairs, and he is forthwith to acquaint his lord, so often as conveniently he may, with the state of his household, and of his treasure and how it is laid forth and what he hath in remain . . .'

Immediately below the Steward came the Comptroller of the Household and the Receiver General or Treasurer. The Gentleman Usher was concerned with 'governing all things above stairs', and his underlings included the

Carver, the Sewer who organised the waiting at table and the seating arrangements, and the gentlemen and yeomen waiters. The Clerk of the Kitchen was responsible for the catering and supply side. He had to 'keep a ledger or journal book for the noting therein weekly the particular expenses of every office, and that book to be summed up at the week's end'. He also had to 'receive all provisions of spice made by the Steward, or Comptroller, and those to keep; fruit, as currants, raisin, prunes, dates, etc. in some reasonable moist place, for else they will dry always, and the dry spices, as sugar, cinnamon, etc. to be kept dry, for that moisture will decay and greatly waste them and so become in time not serviceable'. We can be sure that the kitchen accounts at Hardwick would be carefully inspected week by week, and also that the mistress of the house would want to know why if such expensive provisions as dates, sugar and cinnamon were not kept in perfect condition. The Clerk of the Kitchen controlled the cooks and scullery men, the bakers and brewers, the Yeoman of the Cellar who looked after the wine, the Yeoman of the Buttery who looked after the beer, and the Yeoman of the Pantry who received the bread from the baker and was responsible for bringing the salt and the carving knife and fork to the dinner table.

The Yeoman of the Ewery came under the Steward or the Comptroller. He had charge of the ewers and basins, the candlesticks and table linen, and was responsible for providing the carver with his towel, the master and mistress with their napkins. There were hosts of other functionaries – from the Almoner who dispensed charity to the poor, to the Yeoman of the Wardrobe who looked after the bedding and the comfort of guests; from the Porter who kept the gate (an office of especial importance at Hardwick), to the grooms of the chamber who did the cleaning – but all, from the dignified Steward in his long gown of office down to the half-naked small boys who turned the spits in the seething kitchens, contributed to the smooth running of the great house and represented a whole society in miniature.

Bess of Hardwick herself, whose vision and energy and business acumen had brought this magnificence into being, spent much of her time in her own withdrawing chamber – the Long Gallery being kept for entertaining and for receiving important visitors. But the jewel of the house was undoubtedly the High Great Chamber, or Presence Chamber, which has been described as the most beautiful room in Europe. It was here that Bess could most fully savour her creative triumph. In this room she could feast her eyes on the marvellous frieze, designed and moulded by her own plasterer, Abraham Smith, showing Diana surrounded by her maidens, Venus and Cupid, and over the fireplace the Royal Arms carved in alabaster and black marble. Here, too, Bess could gaze on the superb Brussels tapestries which she herself had chosen, each piece measuring eleven feet deep and exactly filling the space between the wainscot and the frieze. The tapestry in the Presence Chamber tells the story of Ulysses, but Hardwick is full of similar hangings, depicting biblical or classical stories which would soon become familiar to the household – even to those members of it who would never have the skill or inclination to read the originals. The tapestries are works of art and give the great rooms their feeling of richness and luxury. They also served the eminently practical purpose of helping to screen the inmates from the howling draughts of winter on that exposed Derbyshire ridge. Bess herself felt the cold severely – her bed was piled with quilts and no fewer than three pairs of fustian blankets and six woollen blankets. Hardwick must always have been a cold house with its huge expanse of window, but all the same life inside was snug indeed compared with that known by previous generations. The quality of domestic life was steadily improving and becoming rather too comfortable in the opinion of some sturdy citizens who remembered 'the good old days'. 'Our fathers, yea and we ourselves', wrote William Harrison, 'have lain full oft upon straw pallets, on rough mats covered only with a sheet under coverlets made of dagswain, and a good round log under their heads instead of a bolster or pillow. If it were so that our fathers – or the good man of the house had within seven years after his marriage purchased a mattress of flock and a stack of chaff to rest his head upon, he thought himself to be as well lodged as the lord of the town, that peradventure lay seldom in a bed of down or whole feathers. Pillows were then thought meet only for women in childbed. As for servants, if they had any sheet above them, it was well, for seldom had they any under their bodies to keep them from the pricking straws that ran oft through the canvas of the pallet and rased their hardened hides.'

In accordance with custom, Bess's staff was predominantly male, but her 'waiting gentlewomen' were drawn from much the same class as the gentlemen servants. They accompanied their mistress to prayers, helped her to embroider the enormous quantities of coverlets, bedcurtains, hangings and cushions which furnished the rooms and covered every available surface. They read aloud to her and made music for her. Positions of this kind – especially in large, wealthy households – were much sought after by ambitious but dowerless young women. It was, after all, how Bess's own career had started.

As the Countess of Shrewsbury sat now among her ladies, passing a pleasant hour before dinner, surrounded by all the elegance and luxury that money and discerning modern taste could provide, she had every reason to feel satisfied with the success of that career. It was true that her grand-daughter was proving something of a disappointment. There was still no indication whatever that Queen Elizabeth meant to settle the succession on her, and the girl was becoming moody and difficult. But Bess had no doubts about her ability to control Arbella and she had by no means given up hope of living to see her grand-daughter called on to fill the highest place in the land. If Bess had been able to read her grand-daughter's mind during that autumn of 1602, she might have felt rather less complacent about the future.

Arbella, in fact, was rapidly becoming desperate. She had now long passed the normal age for marriage. She would soon have passed the normal age for bearing children. Unless she took matters into her own hands, it looked as if she would languish at Hardwick for ever. Marriage offered the only possible avenue of escape, but first she had to make contact with a prospective bride-groom. John Starkey had proved a disappointment – his fear of the Cavendish family being stronger than Arbella's powers of persuasion – and she had to find another messen-ger. Her choice fell on one of the servants at Hardwick, an elderly man called John Dodderidge. According to the statement made later by Dodderidge: 'About three weeks afore Christmas, as I guess, my Lady Arbella asked me if I would go a little way for her, and I answered I would do the best I could; so she rested for that time. Not long after she told me I must go a hundred miles for her. I made answer that I durst not, for fear of my lady (of Shrews-bury's) displeasure and endangering of my service. She said to me that if I did, I should not need to care, for I should find friends, whereupon I granted that I would go.'

Arbella wanted Dodderidge to approach the Earl of Hertford and re-open the extremely tentative and indirect proposal which had once been made concerning a possible marriage between herself and Hertford's grandson, Edward Seymour, a boy fourteen years younger than Arbella and whom she had never seen. Dodderidge was to go to Hertford's house 'and desire someone of trust about my lord to give you leave to speak with him'. He was on

no account to reveal that Arbella had sent him. If pressed
he could say that he came from her uncles, Henry and
William Cavendish, but whatever happened Hertford
must not be allowed to think that Arbella 'sought the
matter for herself'. When he reached the Earl's presence,
Dodderidge was to say that the question of the marriage
had been considered by the Lady Arbella's friends, who
thought his lordship did not 'take an orderly course' in his
proceedings. It would have been more suitable if Arbella
had been 'first moved in the matter and that the parties
might have had sight the one of the other to see how they
could like'. If Hertford still wanted the match, then he
should send his grandson to Hardwick 'guarded with whom
his lordship thought good'. They must not declare their
business openly, because Bess 'would not seem to deal
in it without the Queen's knowledge' and would be the
first 'shall advertise and complain to the Queen'. Their
best cover story, thought Arbella, would be to say they
had come to sell land or to borrow money. There should
be an older man in the party, so that Edward Seymour
could pose as his son or nephew. This 'grave, ancient
man' could distract Bess's attention by pretending to talk
business, while the young gentleman had 'conference'
with Arbella.

Not surprisingly, Dodderidge was extremely reluctant
to undertake this alarming and complicated mission. He
asked Arbella whether her uncles were really 'acquainted
in the matter or not'. She assured him that they were, and
certainly Henry Cavendish must have known something
about it. Then he wanted to know 'whether there were any
danger in it'. None, said Arbella. If Hertford followed her
instructions, Edward Seymour and his companions would
be able to come and go quite safely, and 'tarry or depart'
as they liked. If anything went wrong, or 'if her Majesty
should not like of it', then the whole affair could be passed
off as 'some money matter'. Anyway, that part of it could

be left to the Earl of Hertford, who was 'wise enough'. Dodderidge was not entirely satisfied, but his objections were ruthlessly overridden. He dared not leave Hardwick without permission, he said. Arbella had thought of that. She would ask one of her grandmother's gentlewomen to get leave for him 'to go into the country to see his friends' and her uncle Henry would provide him with a horse. When Dodderidge protested feebly about his 'unworthiness and insufficiency for delivering of a message to such a one as my lord of Hertford', Arbella told him that all he had to do was to deliver the message and 'it would be entertained at the first'. At the last moment she remembered that Edward Seymour should be told to bring some means of identifying himself, 'whereby it may be known he is the man and to avoid all doubts' – some picture or handwriting of Lady Jane Grey, 'or of the Lady Catherine, or Queen Jane Seymour', anything in fact 'of that family, which we know they, and none but they, have'.

Dodderidge finally set out, much against his better judgement, on Christmas Day, 1602 and Arbella settled down to wait with as much patience as she could muster for the arrival of her knight errant. She could hardly have chosen a more dangerous knight errant, or one more likely to arouse the Queen's worse suspicions. The Earl of Hertford was the same who, as a young man, had secretly married Lady Catherine Grey, and Edward Seymour was Catherine Grey's grandson too. An alliance between the two junior branches of the royal family would create just the kind of situation which those who were working for the peaceful accession of James of Scotland most dreaded.

If Arbella wanted to draw attention to herself she certainly succeeded. She also succeeded in putting an end to her grandmother's peace of mind. The Mistress of Hardwick would soon have to face the fact that her wellordered household was harbouring a determined rebel. Soon, in fact, she would find herself having to do battle

with a resentful, tempestuous young woman – a battle
which was to try the old lady's endurance to its limit.

8 This Unadvised Young Woman

The New Year came in and with it a sense of great changes impending. Nearly half a century had passed since that November morning when a little group of horsemen had taken the road from St James's Palace to Hatfield to tell young Elizabeth Tudor that her sister lay dead and she was Queen of England. Now, incredibly, the Elizabethan era was nearing its end and once again the nation stirred with foreboding for the future. At Hardwick Hall tension mounted as the household listened to the rumours sweeping the countryside, as Arbella Stuart and Bess of Hardwick waited and hoped – Arbella for the young man who would rescue her from a torment of frustration, Bess for news that at last the old Queen had broken the silence of a lifetime and named her successor, named her young cousin Arbella Stuart. For Bess of Hardwick, such news would crown a long and profitable career with triumph. It would set the seal of immortality on the achievements of the yeoman's daughter born eighty-three years ago in the manor farm house barely a stone's throw from the great mansion which flaunted her initials on its turrets, her coat of arms on its façade.

On the 8th of January, 1603, there was a bustle of men and horses in the courtyard at Hardwick and the servants hurried out to welcome an important-looking visitor – a visitor from London who gave orders that his name should be taken up at once to my Lady of Shrewsbury. Bess was walking in the Long Gallery with Arbella and her son William Cavendish when she heard that Sir Henry Brounker had arrived and was asking to see her urgently. Henry Brounker was Robert Cecil's man. Robert Cecil, old Lord Burghley's son, had taken his father's place as the Queen's right-hand man, and was now the most powerful man in England. If Cecil's messenger had made the slow, painful journey to Derbyshire in the dead of winter, then this was – it must surely be – the reward of all her years of hoping and planning and patient scheming. Bess was more than twelve years older than Queen Elizabeth. Unlike the Queen, she was still in the best of health – barring an occasional twinge of rheumatism. She would yet live to see her grand-daughter ascend the English throne.

But when Brounker was ushered into the Gallery, he showed no disposition to go on his knees to Arbella. Instead he greeted Bess with elaborate courtesy, telling her that the Queen wished to be commended to her with all gracious favour. Bess's nerves were so over-wrought that, much to his embarrassment, she attempted to kneel to Sir Henry herself. Hastily preventing such an unsuitable gesture and still keeping up a smooth flow of compliments, he drew the old lady out of earshot of William and Arbella and gave her a letter from the Queen. Whatever that letter contained, it was not what Bess had been expecting. Brounker, watching closely as she read, noticed 'some change of countenance'. Far from offering to make Arbella her heir, it seemed that Elizabeth was seriously displeased with her young kinswoman and had sent Sir Henry Brounker to Hardwick to make a full investigation of the matter. Brounker was now asking for permission to speak to Arbella in private – permission which, he reported, was 'easily granted'.

Bess was too dazed with disappointment and alarm to make any resistance. As she stood with the Queen's letter in her hand, it was as if the ground had suddenly opened under her feet. What could Arbella have been doing to bring not good news, but an ominously implied threat from London? It was true she had shown signs recently of resenting the nun-like seclusion of her life, but Bess had kept such a careful watch over her, day and night. She found it hard to believe that the girl could have been so foolish as to endanger the brilliant future which lay now in such delicate balance.

Meanwhile, Brounker was confronting Arbella at the other end of the Gallery. He began by assuring her that the Queen wished her well, sent thanks for her New Year's gift and would be glad to hear how she did. Then, circuitously, he approached the point of his mission. He had to 'break a matter' which the Queen had taken unkindly, especially considering how ready she would have been at any time to have yielded to any of Arbella's reasonable desires, if only she had been told of them. But although Arbella had been deceitful, there was still an 'open way' by which she could give the Queen a 'great testimony of her integrity'. If she would truly and sincerely impart 'all the particular circumstances of the matter', how it had proceeded and who she had used in it – a matter which was already so well known and so openly confessed that there was no denying it – she would show 'her desire to repair any error committed by her'. Naturally Arbella would be eager to take this opportunity to make amends, unless, of course, she wanted Elizabeth to believe that in her action she had laid aside the duty and affection she owed to the Queen, 'both as her subject and of her blood'.

During this classic opening to a Tudor interrogation Brounker noticed 'by the coming and going of her colour', that Arbella seemed 'somewhat troubled'. Unlike her grandmother, Arbella had been able to guess only too accurately what had brought Sir Henry to Hardwick. All the same, after a little pause, she was ready with an equally classic response. She was 'much grieved' that the Queen should have conceived an ill opinion of her, but if Brounker would tell her what offence she was supposed to have committed, then she would answer truly and either justify herself or confess her fault.

Brounker was far too old a hand to fall for that one. Did not her own conscience accuse her of 'any late undutifulness' he enquired? But no, Arbella would not acknowledge 'so much as a thought' to offend the Queen. Sir Henry began to press home the attack. Had she not had some 'intelligence with the Earl of Hertford' and employed a man to go to him? Again Arbella 'denied all'. Then, said Brounker coldly, she failed 'both in duty and judgement'. It was not strange for a young lady to err, he went on persuasively. What had passed could not be recalled, but it might yet be amended with repentance and plain dealing. Brounker would be glad if Arbella would 'so carry herself as it might appear her offence to proceed of vanity and love of herself, rather than want of duty and contempt of her Majesty'. He begged her 'to remember herself before she waded too far in this course of wilfulness'. She would have to confess in the end, far better if she did so willingly at the first.

On the face of it, Arbella's 'crime' does not seem especially serious. It was natural enough that a healthy young woman of twenty-seven should have been desperate to escape from her grandmother's relentless surveillance and enjoy some life of her own. But for anyone of the blood royal – particularly one who stood as near to the throne as Arbella – to embark on marriage plans without the Queen's consent was playing with fire. Forty years before, Lady Catherine Grey's defiance had resulted in life imprisonment. Arbella knew this as she did her best to outface Henry Brounker.

His next question told her how slim were her chances of success. Did she know one Dodderidge? he asked. If the Queen and the Council knew about Dodderidge, then they probably knew it all. Obviously something had gone badly wrong, but Arbella still managed to keep up an appearance of indifference. Yes, she knew Dodderidge well and had last seen him before Christmas. She thought he was now with his friends in Berkshire.

Brounker felt the time had come to play his ace. Typically enough, Arbella had never considered the most probable effect of her ingenuous message upon the Earl of Hertford who, as Catherine Grey's unauthorised husband, had spent a large part of his life under the shadow of royal displeasure. When John Dodderidge had brought him an open invitation to run his head into the noose a second time, the Earl had not hesitated for a moment. Dodderidge found his 'entertainment' very different from the one he had so optimistically been promised. The unfortunate messenger had been bundled out of Hertford's presence and shut up by himself to write out a full account of the affair. On the following day, he had been brought before Robert Cecil by a badly frightened Hertford. Henry Brounker had brought his confession to Hardwick, and now he produced it from his pouch. He could draw the matter at length, he told Arbella, and 'trouble her with many questions', but 'seeing she was resolved to be wilful' he would show her something 'against which there could be no exception'.

Arbella recognised Dodderidge's handwriting at once. Obviously there was no point in further denials, but she did not surrender immediately. Something might yet be saved from the wreck of her plans. It was true, she admitted, that she had once had a meaning to send Dodderidge to the Earl of Hertford, but 'upon better advice' she had revoked her instructions. Anyway, Dodderidge was 'a bold, lewd fellow' who would do anything for gain. It was no use. Brounker pressed home his advantage and finally Arbella broke down, but 'so confusedly and with words so far from the purpose' that Sir Henry could make nothing of it. She would do well to deal plainly, he said sternly. She could not have been alone in a matter of such importance, and therefore every person concerned in the business must be made known. Arbella promised that she would 'deal plainly and sincerely' but first Brounker must promise to conceal it from her grandmother. Brounker, who knew something of Bess's reputation, could sympathise with this request and agreed to the bargain, but only on condition that 'all might be set down in writing' and nothing left to his report.

Feeling that he had done enough for one day, Brounker left Arbella alone to write her confession – she might prove more forthcoming and more coherent on paper. He kept his promise not to tell Bess anything about his errand and she was left in agonising suspense, not knowing whether all her hopes for 'her jewel Arbelle' were now in ruins, or even whether her grand-daughter was in imminent danger of arrest on a charge of treason. Queen Elizabeth might be growing old, her physical powers might be failing, but with her own personal experience of the Queen's wrath in the past, the Countess of Shrewsbury had no illusions about her continued ability to strike if it were even suspected that Arbella was involved in a plot to seize the throne. Bess had no illusions either about the likely reactions of the rival heir, whose claim to the succession, even she had to admit, was rather better than Arbella's. King James of Scotland, now a vigorous, self-opinionated man of thirty-six, had been waiting more or less impatiently for the last fifteen years to be recognised as Elizabeth's heir. He would show no mercy to anyone who made a bungling attempt to cheat him of so rich a prize as the English crown. While she waited for somebody to tell her what was going on under her own roof, Bess could only pace the exquisite, tapestried rooms of Hardwick – outwardly as erect and formidable as ever, inwardly afraid to the marrow of her old bones.

When Brounker read Arbella's confession, he was seriously disappointed, finding it to be 'confused, obscure and in truth ridiculous'. It was not a letter fit for him to carry, he told her, nor for the Queen to read. She would have to try again. But her second effort turned out to be little better than the first. It contained none of the names and details the government would be expecting. In fact, the only explanation Arbella seemed able to offer for her 'disobedience' was that she had wanted to reach the Queen's presence and, despairing of getting her grandmother's permission for even such 'a small ordinary liberty', had chosen this roundabout method of achieving her object. Brounker really began to wonder if she was quite right in the head – whether perhaps 'her wits were somewhat distracted either with fear of her grandmother or conceit of her own folly'. But after some more fruitless sessions with the tearful young woman who seemed ready to tell him everything except what he wanted to hear, he decided the time had come to take Bess into his confidence. It was a painful interview. 'The old lady', reported Brounker, 'was wonderfully afflicted with the matter and much discomforted'. Although he assured her again and again of the Queen's favour and 'gracious good opinion of her faithfulness' which, he said, he had heard from Elizabeth's own mouth, Bess 'took it so ill as with much ado she refrained her hands'.

Brounker's visit to Hardwick prolonged itself over several days, while he struggled to soothe Bess's rage and alarm and to extract some sense out of Arbella's flow of verbiage. Finally, exasperated by her 'often and idle writing' and 'to conclude this endless business', he had yielded to her entreaties to set down what he would and she would subscribe it. He therefore made 'a collection of all the particulars wherewith she was charged' which Arbella 'willingly confessed' and humbly begged the Queen's pardon for all her offences. Difficult though she had been, Brounker seems to have felt a certain sneaking sympathy for Arbella. She had been led astray, he thought, 'abused' by base companions who had made her believe that the Earl of Hertford would welcome her overtures. As a hard-headed man of the world, he probably found it impossible to take her monumental ineptitude very seriously. He had not found 'any strange company' at Hardwick or any evidence of a dangerous conspiracy.

When at last Brounker took his leave, Bess attempted, perhaps not very wisely, 'to fasten a purse full of gold' on to him in honour of the Queen. Sir Henry virtuously refused to accept a gift which might have been interpreted as a bribe and rode away from the seething atmosphere of the great house with what can only have been a profound sense of relief. He was not to know that he had by no means seen the last of Hardwick.

The strain of the past few days and the shock of discovering that her docile, dutiful little grand-daughter had turned into a passionate woman who would apparently stop at nothing to get her own way, had left Bess physically and emotionally exhausted. But before she could allow herself the luxury of a rest, there was something she had to do. Calling for pen and paper, she sat down to write a letter to the Queen.

'Most gracious sovereign. I cannot sufficiently in words express the infinite and great comfort I have continually received by your Majesty's most princely favours to me and now by your most gracious letter and message sent by Sir Henry Brounker, who will particularly inform your Majesty of all things here ... These matters were unexpected of me, being altogether ignorant of Arbell's vain doings, as on my salvation and allegiance to your Majesty I protest. Notwithstanding her vanity, I rest most certain of her loyal and dutiful mind to your Majesty. But seeing she hath been content to hear matters of any moment and not to impart them to me, I am desirous and most humbly beseech your Majesty that she may be placed elsewhere, to learn to be more considerate, and after that it may please your Majesty either to accept of her service about your royal person or to bestow her in marriage, which in all humility and duty I do crave ... for I cannot now assure myself of her as I have done.'

It was a hard decision to take – virtually to disown the much-loved 'jewel' round whom the dreams of half a life-time had been woven, but Bess of Hardwick had not risen to pre-eminence in her generation by shirking hard decisions. Seventy years had passed since she had left her father's house at the age of twelve to seek her fortune in a world which gave no quarter to the weak and shiftless – a world where only the strong and fortunate survived. Bess had fought her way to the top by her own brains and guts and will-power. She had little sympathy to spare for those who shrank in the face of adversity or who gambled away their chances by futile scheming. Arbella had disappointed her bitterly and put at risk everything she had worked so hard to achieve, but Bess of Hardwick had never given way under danger or disappointment. She would not give way now.

9 Royal Prisoner

After studying Brounker's report, Robert Cecil came to the comforting conclusion that Arbella did not represent any serious danger to his plans. But Cecil, who had staked his political future on accomplishing the peaceful transference of power to James of Scotland, was particularly anxious to avoid a scandal at this stage and 'idle talks and rumours, whereof there is aptness in most men to take liberty at this time'. Officially, therefore, Arbella's regrettable lapse was ascribed to those convenient 'base companions' who, 'thinking it pleasing to her youth and sex to be sought in marriage', had attempted for devious purposes of their own to lead her astray 'with a device that the Earl of Hertford had a purpose to match his grandchild with her'. Arbella was, however, to be warned that in future she must 'content herself to live in good sort with so dear a parent and so worthy a matron' as the Dowager Countess of Shrewsbury. If she dabbled in 'such like plots and practices' again, she might not get off so lightly, for 'being of that blood she is, her Majesty will look for an extraordinary account of her proceedings'. Cecil was also anxious to avoid promoting the impression that Arbella was a prisoner in case it encouraged rescue attempts, and he instructed Bess to 'avoid any such manner of guarding your house, or excluding resort, as may continue the fond bruits that are raised'. He quite understood that Bess, because of her age and sickness, could not be always in her grand-daughter's company but, he suggested hopefully, she might 'impose some care upon some discreet gentlewoman ... and some honest gentlemen to attend her amongst the rest, who, without using any extraordinary restraint, may have eyes sufficiently unto her if she do anything unfit for her, either in duty to the Queen or in prejudice of her own honour or well-doing'. 'To conclude, Madame', he wrote, 'we must again reiterate unto you her Majesty's gracious acceptation of your dutiful care and affection to please her. Only you must receive this answer for your suit to be freed of her (Arbella), that her Majesty cannot think of any other place so fit for her as this is, and therefore desireth you to remain contented and to look to your health that God may give you a comfortable life, which her Majesty wisheth you as much as any friend you have.'

If Cecil hoped he had now disposed of the problem of Arbella, he had greatly underestimated her tenacity and the desperation of her resolve to escape from Hardwick whatever the cost. She now began openly to defy her grandmother and to drop hints about a mysterious 'lover'. Bess's next letter to the Queen, dated January 29th, shows how rapidly their relationship had deteriorated. 'I understand some part of your Highness' pleasure touching this unadvised young woman here, and do most humbly desire that I may know your Majesty's further pleasure . . . I will not respect my trouble or charge to do your Majesty any service that shall lie in me during life, but I doubt it is not in my power now to do that service to your Majesty in this matter as I desire, for the bad persuasions of some have so estranged her mind and natural affection from me that she holds me the greatest enemy she hath, and hath given herself over to be ruled and advised by others, so that, the bond of nature being broken, I cannot have any assurance of her good carriage. I cannot but doubt there is another match in working, but who the party should be, I cannot conjecture . . . She is borne in hand, as I gather, that she shall have your Majesty's good liking and allowance of anything she doth, and have liberty to have resort to her and herself to go or ride at her own pleasure. For my own part, I should have little care how meanly soever she were bestowed so as it were not offensive to your

Highness. So far as my credit doth extend with her, I advise her to attempt nothing without your Majesty's pleasure first known. She saith she will do all duty to your Majesty, but desireth me to forbear to examine her. Her vain speech puts further doubts into me of her folly . . . Sometimes she will say that she can be taken away off my hands if she will . . .'

When Cecil's letter reached Hardwick and Arbella realised that the government did not intend to remove her from her grandmother's custody, she composed a long letter to Bess, promising to set down the 'true reasons' for her approach to Hertford. This 'declaration fraught with vanity' was promptly forwarded to Cecil by Bess. 'Such as it is, I have sent it hereinclosed', she wrote, 'but I could not by any possible means prevail with her to set down the matter plainly, as I desired she would in few lines. These strange courses are wonderful to me, and cannot but greatly grieve me . . .' Bess no longer knew what to make of Arbella. 'What truth there is in this new matter, I know not', she wrote. 'It may be the matter is not so far proceeded as she makes show, and that it is but a practice as the former was, but I cannot but doubt the worst.'

Arbella's letter was full of references to her 'dearest and best trusted'. 'As I may compare the love of this worthy gentleman (which I have already unreservedly accepted and confirmed and will never deny nor repent, whatsoever befall)', she wrote, 'to gold which hath been so often purified that I cannot find one fault, jealousy only excepted, so I have dealt unkindly, shrewdly, proudly with him, and if any living have cause to think me proud or shrewish, it is he whom I have loved too well (ever since I could love) to hide any word, thought or deed of mine from him, unless it were to awe him a little when I thought his love converted into hate.' No wonder Bess was alarmed and mystified. According to Arbella, it was this 'worthy gentleman' who had urged her to approach the Earl of Hertford.

He had taught her 'by the example of Samuel that one might plead one errand and deliver another with a safe conscience'. He had assured her that the Queen's offence 'would be converted into laughter, when her Majesty should see the honest cunning of the contriver'. 'He told me he would have me enter into some great action', she went on, 'to win myself reputation, try her Majesty's love to me, though neither of us doubted of it, try what my friends would do for me, and how I could employ my friends and servants.' Arbella was not ashamed of her choice, she could find it in her heart to reveal his name, but dared not without his consent.

On February 6th Bess was writing to Cecil again. Arbella had now agreed 'to make the party's name she favoureth known to her Majesty by any that shall please her Highness to send hither'. But 'for that Sir Henry Brounker hath been employed before in these matters, her humble suit is that he may be sent again'. Matters were, in fact, building to a crisis. Towards the end of the month Arbella became ill 'with extreme pain of her side', so that Bess 'was in great fear for her'. A 'doctor of physic' had been summoned but, wrote Bess, 'I see her mind is the cause of all'. This letter is dated February 21st but before it was despatched Bess was obliged to add a postscript. 'Arbell is so wilfully bent that she hath made a vow not to eat or drink in this house at Hardwick, or where I am, till she may hear from her Majesty, so that for preservation of her life I am enforced to suffer her to go to a house of mine called Oldcotes, two miles from here. I am wearied of my life and therefore humbly beseech her Majesty to have compassion on me. And I earnestly pray you to send Sir Henry Brounker hither.'

So once more Sir Henry Brounker took the road to Derbyshire and at the beginning of March he once more confronted Arbella at Hardwick. He brought with him a long list of questions, based on her own letter to Bess, and all designed to uncover the identity of her mysterious gentleman friend. But when Arbella found that Brounker had not come to take her away, she deliberately obstructed the interrogation. Every time she was asked who the 'noble gentleman' was who had tried to win her love, she would only answer 'the King of Scots'. Eventually, of course, she broke down in tears and was obliged to admit that the noble gentleman had no existence outside her own imagination. Brounker got a written declaration from her which began: 'I take Almighty God to witness, I am free from promise, contract, marriage, or intention to marry, and so mean to be whilst I live.' She withdrew all her boasts about her 'lover' and added pathetically that experience had taught her that there was no other way of getting the Queen to take some notice of her 'but by incurring some suspicion and having no ground to work but this, and this being love'. But if the Queen would only show her some favour and grant her her 'dear and due liberty' she would make a solemn vow never to marry while she lived.

Brounker left Hardwick the following day, carrying with him yet another letter from Bess to Cecil in which she apologised for having wasted his messenger's time and begging once again that Arbella should be speedily removed. 'She is so wilfully bent and there is so little reason in most of her doings, that I cannot tell what to make of it. A few more weeks as I have suffered of late', added the old lady, 'will make an end of me.' As for Arbella, when her second attempt at escape ended in failure, she lost her head completely and began to bombard Brounker in London with long, rambling, incoherent letters – so much so that certain people began seriously to doubt her sanity.

If Arbella hoped to move the Council by her endless scribbling, she was mistaken. Robert Cecil remained implacable in his determination to keep her safely out of the way at Hardwick. He instructed Bess to deal mildly with her grand-daughter, 'howsoever she may offend you in this time of her passion'. He also asked that she should, if possible, be prevented from sending any more of her 'strange and inconvenient letters'. But Arbella's flow was unstoppable and Bess's patience, after weeks of intense nervous strain, had reached its limit. Soon violent scenes between the old woman and the young re-echoed through the high tapestried rooms and galleries. Bess, followed by William Cavendish, had burst in on Arbella while she 'sat scribbling till twelve of the clock at night' and hurled volleys of 'most bitter and injurious words' at her. Arbella, battered she wrote by a 'contemptible storm of threatenings', fled down to the great chamber to find a messenger to carry her latest tale of woe to Brounker. The household had been warming themselves at the fire and no doubt listening fascinated to the sounds of battle raging above, but when Arbella appeared they drew away. All the same, she found one young man 'who stood with his hat in his hand and my glove in his hat' ready to be 'my undaunted and most trusty servant'.

There was open war now at Hardwick, but in the Palace at Richmond Queen Elizabeth lay dying and the air was thick with rumour and speculation about the future. The Venetians, in particular, were receiving almost daily reports. '. . . The Queen is said to be very sick. Arbella is diversely reported of and is like to be sent up shortly to be guarded . . .' '. . . Lady Arbella is under guard, some say married to the Earl of Hertford's grandchild, which is most false; some that she is mad . . .' '. . . The Queen's sickness continues, and every man's head is full of proclamations as to what shall become of us afterwards.' 'The marriage of Lady Arbella is discussed every day with greater freedom, and especially are the minds of the Kings of France and Spain well disposed towards her, for neither one nor the other would willingly see a single sovereign in England, Scotland and Ireland.

The King of Scotland, as a male and senior to Arbella, has the favour of the people, but he lives surrounded by conspiracies which threaten his death . . .' 'All minds are anxious and the partisans of the King of Scotland, in order to destroy public sympathy for Arbella, are spreading reports prejudicial to her character as an honest woman . . .'

On Thursday, March 10th, came the attempt to rescue Arbella which Bess had dreaded for so long. 'About twelve of the clock', she reported to Brounker later that same day, 'Arbell came out of her chamber, went towards the gates (as she said) intending to walk, but, being persuaded it was dinner time, did stay. About two of the clock in the afternoon, there came to my gates my son Henry Cavendish and one Mr Stapleton . . . For that Arbell was desirous to speak with my bad son Henry, I was content to suffer him to come into my house and speak with her, rather than she to go to him, but sent him word not to remain here above two hours. I would not suffer Stapleton to come within my gates, for I have disliked him of long for many respects . . . Arbell and Henry Cavendish had not talked as I think a dozen words together but they both came down and offered to go out of my gates. One of my servants entreated them not to offer to go out until they had my consent. Arbell seemed unwilling to stay, yet at length by persuasion did stay till word was brought to me. When I understood of it, I sent to her that I did not think it good she should speak with Stapleton, and wished her to forbear it . . . She asked if she were a prisoner, and said she would see, and so went to the gates and would have gone out, but was not suffered. Yet she did speak to Stapleton, looking through the gates, some vain, idle words of salutation . . . So with much sending to Stapleton to depart, at length he went from my gates. She had appointed Henry Cavendish to come hither again tomorrow, which I forbade, and so I think he will not come. He was no sooner gone out of my gates but she made herself ready to walk abroad, which I thought not convenient she should do and so she stayed.'

Arbella's uncle Henry and Stapleton, 'a very wilful Papist', had forty well-armed horsemen with them who might easily have overpowered the garrison at Hardwick – but Bess's indomitable will had prevailed. She thought it 'not convenient' that Arbella should go, and so she stayed. Bess had saved Arbella from courting certain and complete disaster, but the old lady could do no more. She was very tired and prayed yet again that Arbella should be removed.

Henry Brounker, no doubt cursing women in general and Arbella in particular, made his way north for the third time in three months to investigate the situation on the spot. He found Hardwick in a state of siege with relations between Bess and Arbella at breaking point. 'The Lady Arbella hath neither altered her speech nor behaviour,' he told Robert Cecil. 'She is certain in nothing but her uncertainty. She justifieth herself and desireth liberty. I persuade her to patience and conformity, but nothing will satisfy her but her remove from her grandmother, so settled is her mislike of the old lady, upon what ground I cannot conceive, unless it be upon the restraint of messengers and letters which minister occasion of much writing, to the distempering of her brains, apparent enough by the multitude of her idle discourses which your lordships have lately seen.'

Brounker's sympathies were by this time entirely with Bess. 'The old lady groweth exceeding weary of her charge', he wrote. 'She beginneth to be weak and sickly by breaking her sleep, and cannot long continue this vexation.' Sir Henry was also fully alive to the dangers of the situation which had been allowed to develop at Hardwick. 'Every man's mouth is full of the Queen's danger, and Arbella receives daily advertisements to that purpose . . . I suppose her wilfulness, which is much greater and more peremptory than before, ariseth out of a hope of the Queen's death. I find her so vain and idle as I seldom trouble her, neither doth she much desire my company, though I pretended I came to see her wrongs righted and to compound all matters between her grandmother and her.' Brounker did not feel competent to deliver judgement on the 'late assembly' at Hardwick until he had been able to make further enquiries, but he was convinced that something positive would have to be done about Arbella. 'I am verily persuaded', he wrote, 'that her remove only will stay her practice, which I perceive is resolved by herself and others. If her Majesty should miscarry . . . I do not see how she can be kept in this place two days, and therefore it were good that her remove were thought on in time, if her escape may breed danger.'

As a result of Brounker's recommendations, Arbella was at last removed from Bess's care. If her only object had been escape from Hardwick, she had got her way, though at the cost of much reputation and personal dignity. If, as Henry Brounker evidently believed, she had intended to make a bid for the throne on her own account, she could scarcely have made a more disastrous mess of things. On March 22nd she was taken to Wrest Park in Bedfordshire, the house of the Earl of Kent whose nephew had married her cousin Elizabeth Talbot, and Bess was left in peace. Hardwick was quiet once more but the sense of urgency had gone. No more messengers slipped in and out of its gates – no more muddied, weary horsemen rode across the courtyard – Bess no longer needed to guard against potential kidnappers and conspirators or to see mysterious strangers lurking behind every bush. It was all a little dull.

10 When Hardwick Towers Shall Bow Their Head

Queen Elizabeth died very peacefully in the early hours of Thursday, March 24th, 1603. Her last conscious act had been to name her 'cousin of Scotland' to succeed her. Elizabeth had reigned over England for forty-four years, four months and seven days – far longer than any other monarch since the days of Edward III – and the great majority of her subjects could not remember the world without her, for many of them it would never be the same place again.

Although the news of the Queen's death sped northward as the couriers posted for life up the road to Scotland, it would have been some weeks before the details of her passing reached Hardwick and by that time James was already on his way south to take up his inheritance. Nobody had mentioned Arbella Stuart. Sir Robert Cecil had won. Bess of Hardwick would never see her granddaughter proclaimed Queen – the dreams of nearly thirty years had vanished within a matter of weeks. But Bess had never wasted time and energy regretting what might have been. She would be eighty-three on her next birthday, a very great age, but she remained remarkably fit and active. All the same, not even Bess was immortal and the time was coming when she must set her affairs in order.

'I, Elizabeth, Countess of Shrewsbury, lately wife of George, Earl of Shrewsbury deceased; having learned as well out of the holy Word of God, as by the common experience of the world, that all flesh must change this mortal life, and that the hour and time of death is most uncertain and not to be known to any mortal creature . . . do now by this my writing, in my perfect health and good memory, ordain and make this my last Will and Testament; as well to have my mind quiet from all worldly respects . . . as also to prevent all suits, debates and controversy that otherwise may arise or be moved amongst my children, whom I most chiefly desire and heartily pray to live in all unity and natural affection.'

In her Will, first drawn up in April 1601, Bess left Chatsworth to her eldest son, Henry, and Hardwick and Oldcotes to William. Arbella, then 'her very loving grandchild', was to receive: 'My crystal glass framed with silver and gilt, and set with lapis lazarus and agate; and one sable, the head being of gold set with stone, and a white ermine sable, the head being of gold enamelled; and all my pearls and jewels, which I shall have at my decease, except such as shall be otherwise bequeathed by this my last Will; and I shall give to her a thousand pounds in money.' But by the spring of 1603, the situation had changed. Bess had not forgiven her 'bad son Henry' for his part in encouraging Arbella's revolt or for attempting to rescue her grand-daughter from Hardwick by force. Nor had she forgiven Arbella. Two days before Arbella finally left Hardwick, the old lady had added a codicil to her Will. 'Forasmuch as I have changed my mind touching my bequests and legacies to my grand-daughter Arbella Stuart, and my son Henry Cavendish; I have fully determined and resolved that neither my said grand-daughter, nor the said Henry Cavendish, or either of them, shall have any benefit by any such gift or legacy. I therefore declare by this codicil, that every gift or legacy by me appointed to them, be utterly frustrate, void and of none effect.'

Bess was now able to enjoy Hardwick as a thing of beauty, undistracted by her responsibilities for Arbella. Two years earlier, with typical thoroughness, she had embarked on the mammoth task of compiling an inventory of the contents of the house which she was anxious should remain in their proper setting. She left her grandson, the second William Cavendish, a cup of lapis lazarus with a cover to it, all garnished with gold, enamelled 'as an heirloom to go with her house at Hardwick'. All the furniture at Hardwick was entailed; 'because' wrote Bess, 'it hath pleased God to give me leave to perform some buildings at my houses at Chatsworth, Hardwick and Oldcotes in the county of Derby, which I greatly desire should be well preserved and the furniture continued at my said houses for the better furnishing thereof, into whose possession soever, of my blood, the said houses shall come'.

The passage of nearly four centuries has scattered many of Bess's treasures, yet some of the items listed in the inventory do still remain. In the High Great Chamber the 'six pieces of fair tapestry hangings of the story of Ulysses, eleven foot deep' still line the walls of that marvellous room which was designed to hold them. 'A drawing table carved and gilt standing upon sea dogs inlaid with marble stones and wood' is also still at Hardwick. But the carpet for it 'of needlework of the story of David and Saul with a gold fringe and trimmed with blue taffeta sarcenet' has succumbed to the ravages of time and moth. Two of the inlaid tables survive – one being the famous walnut table made for that long ago triple Shrewsbury wedding: Talbot arms impaling Hardwick, Cavendish impaling Talbot. Another piece of furniture listed by Bess and which would remind her of her fourth and most brilliant marriage every time she looked at it, was the chest of oak and walnut and marquetry, with two arcaded panels inlaid with distant buildings seen through an arch. The keystones of the arches bear the initials G.T. which may be George Talbot or Gilbert his son. The chest itself has drawers in the lower section – an innovation which represents an early stage in the evolution of that useful object, the chest of drawers.

Wandering from the Presence or High Great Chamber into the Long Gallery, Bess could feast her eyes on the so-called Gideon tapestries, her pleasure no doubt increased by the satisfactory knowledge that they had been a bargain. She had acquired them second-hand from the Hatton family in 1592 when she had been in London on a shopping spree for Hardwick. The thirteen pieces of arras 'containing one thousand ells and a half of arras of the story of Gideon' had cost her £326 . 15 . 9d. 'Whereof for making of new arms was abated five pounds.' Bess paid Mr Sheldon's man thirty shillings and fourpence for changing the Hatton coat of arms to Hardwick, while the Hatton does were converted into Cavendish stags by the simple expedient of adding horns. Bess also bought 'four pieces of arras of the story of Abraham, every piece twelve foot deep' from the Hattons. In the Inventory these are referred to as a second set of hangings for the withdrawing chamber.

The Inventory is an astonishing document. Every chair, every stool, every cushion, table cover and carpet is listed. Everything is covered in needlework in blue and crimson, orange tawny, green and purple – everything embellished with gold and silver and silk fringe. But the practical Bess was not merely concerned with counting her valuables – the looking glass decorated with mother of pearl and silver; the great gilt salt cellar weighing sixty-two ounces; another salt of gold and crystal weighing five and a half ounces; the cups and ewers and basins of gold and parcel gilt. She also lists spare ticks for feather beds, chamber pots, a frying pan, a collander, blankets and coverlets, kitchen candlesticks, bolsters, kettles and fire-irons – all the paraphernalia, in fact, of daily life four hundred years ago.

As well as taking housewifely care to leave her worldly possessions in good order, Bess, after the fashion of her time and class, was making other methodical preparations for eternity. 'I commend and commit my soul into the hands of my most merciful and heavenly Father, most humbly beseeching him, and faithfully believing that he will place the same in the most blessed company of his

Elect, there most comfortably to praise his Holy Name for ever more; and my body I commit to the earth, whereof it came, and to be buried in Allhallows Church in Derby, in the place of the same church where it is appointed and determined that my tomb shall be erected and built, which at this present is finished and wanteth nothing but setting up. And I especially will and require that my funeral be not over sumptuous, or otherwise performed with too much vain and idle charge; requiring only that it may be accomplished in decent and convenient order, fit for that estate and degree to which it hath pleased my most merciful God to prefer me.' Bess was leaving nothing to chance and paid a visit to All Saints Church to inspect her last resting place, the foundations for which had cost her seven pounds, fifteen shillings and sixpence.

Bess had always been good to her dependants. Throughout her life she had performed many thoughtful acts of charity and in her closing years had endowed an almshouse at Derby for 'the perpetual relief of eight poor men and four poor women', who were to be of 'good and honest conversation and not infected with any contagious disease'. Being Bess, all the arrangements were extremely businesslike down to the last details. 'The said new admitted poor shall receive one cognizance or badge of silver of the Almshouses, and one bedstead, one mattress, one bolster, two pairs of sheets, two coffers, two tables, one cupboard, two stools, four pewter dishes, iron tongs, fire shovel, and all the furniture of every several room by written indenture subscribed by the Warden or one of the bailiffs.' The inmates were daily to 'keep his or her lodging clean with sweeping and the furniture in decent and honest manner'. There was to be no going absent without leave, no playing truant from prayers. Those who could work were to do so and not haunt alehouses or keep bad company. There was to be no brawling or tippling, and persistent offenders could be expelled.

Bess installed a Warden, one Richard Hayward and his wife Dorothy, and she had devised a way of putting her endowment to practical use. 'The said Richard Hayward during his life, and always after his death, the Warden of the said Almshouses shall have and keep the key of the upper part of the quire or chancel of the Church of All Saints; where the said Countess meaneth to have her tomb or monument placed, and shall at least every week, once or oftener, as need shall require, cleanse, dust and sweep over the said monument, and the place about it, from all dust and annoyance upon or about the same.' The inmates of the almshouse were also to parade in the church twice a day, winter and summer, to pray before the tomb of their foundress.

Bess's closing years passed peacefully. She continued to take a lively interest in the world about her. A regular correspondent in London kept her informed of the latest gossip, and news of Arbella, now spreading her wings at Court, reached Hardwick from time to time. Arbella, who was finding Court life expensive, paid a visit to her grandmother in 1605 and got a somewhat chilly reception. The old lady relented sufficiently to present her with a gold cup worth a hundred pounds and £300 in cash, but she was not reinstated in the Will. Bess cannot be said to have mellowed greatly with age, although she did make up her quarrel with her step-son, Gilbert Talbot and her daughter Mary. The Shrewsburys and Charles Cavendish visited Hardwick in December, 1607, where, according to Gilbert, they found 'a lady of great years, of great wealth, and of great wit, which yet still remains. She received us with all respect and affection, and stayed us with her one day . . . without so much as one word of any former suits or unkindness, but only compliment, courtesy and kindness.'

Bess was now eighty-seven – an almost unheard of age for her times – and to her descendants must have begun to seem as much a permanent part of the landscape as the houses she had built. But Gilbert Talbot noticed a great change in her. 'She did eat very little and was not able to walk the length of the chamber betwixt two, but grew so ill at it as you might plainly discern.' On New Year's Day, 1608 she was reported as looking 'pretty well' and speaking 'heartily', but it was obvious now that the end could not be long delayed. Bess took to her bed and Mrs Digby, her personal maid, sent a message to Gilbert telling him that 'her ladyship was so ill she could not be from her day nor night'. Bess's wonderful physique was failing at last, but she still retained 'the blessing of sense and memory'. 'Within the space of twenty days next before her death' she gave her executor William, now Baron Cavendish, various additional instructions. He was to invest the sum of one hundred pounds and use the profits to pay for any necessary repairs at the almshouse in Derby. Because her daughter and son-in-law and Charles Cavendish, 'by their means', had previously offered her 'unkindness' Bess had left them nothing but blessings in her Will. Now she told William that she 'would have him give to her daughter Shrewsbury, from her, the Pearl Bed with all that belonged to it in that chamber, except the hangings'. She also gave 'unto her son Charles Cavendish four thousand marks for him to bestow in land for his two sons'. Faithful Mrs Digby was to have a hundred pounds. Bess remembered that Mr Clay of Crich owed her a hundred pounds. Clay could keep fifty of it, she told William, and give the other fifty to his daughter Mary. All the loose ends were tied up at last. There was nothing more to be done but to die decently and in good order, devoutly calling on God 'whilst she had breath'.

A legend was to grow up in the Cavendish family that Bess had been told she would never die while she was still building. It was bitterly cold that winter. The Thames froze, birds dropped dead from the trees and, so it is said, a message came from the site of Bess's latest project that work was impossible. She is supposed to have given orders that ale was to be heated to boiling point and used to mix the mortar, but in vain, and when the old lady heard this, she turned her face to the wall and died. It is a nice story, but Bess was not building anywhere in 1608. Oldcotes, her last house, had been finished nine years before. In any case, the facts of Bess are more stupendous than any fable. As she lay dying, she could look back on a lifespan and a record of achievement unrivalled among her contemporaries. Without any initial advantages of birth, influence or fortune she had carved out a brilliant business career in an age when competition for power and position was fierce and the penalties of failure were harsh. She had been a buyer and seller of land, a moneylender and a financier, a farmer, a merchant of lead and coal and timber. She had become an extremely rich woman. She had allied her family to the royal house of England.

It had not been easy. Bess had known sorrow and disappointment and fear. She had felt the consequences of royal displeasure, suffered from the malice of enemies and the squalid aftermath of a broken marriage. But always she had held her head high as she marched resolutely forward from one goal to the next. Bess had never asked for favours, never given way to self-pity. She has been described as 'proud, furious, selfish and unfeeling', as 'a bitter shrew', as being insatiable in her lust for money, power and possessions. Certainly she had always driven a hard bargain and spared little sympathy or understanding for those weaker than herself; but according to her own lights she had dealt justly and honestly and always drove herself as hard as she drove others.

And now none of it mattered any more – the dynasty she had founded, the empire she had created, the great houses she had built, the royal grand-daughter on whom she had pinned such hopes. Bess was slipping out on the ebb tide, away from the stifling, luxurious room she lay in, the ring of eager, watchful faces, the chaplain droning his prayers at her bedside. What did she see in the shadows closing over her – her eyes turned inward now on the long pageant of her life. The four husbands she had outlived – young Robert Barlow who had died so long ago? William Cavendish whose children she had born and striven for and from whom were to spring a line of dukedoms? William St Loe who had loved her; George, Earl of Shrewsbury who had come to hate her? Did she see Mary Queen of Scots, glittering, devious and dangerous; or the little Arbella, plump and docile at her lessons, learning to be a Queen under her grandmother's eye – Arbella whose final tragedy was now fast approaching, doomed since her birth, doomed by her own blood? Or did she see perhaps that other little girl who had set out so hopefully to seek her fortune in the great wide world?

Bess died on February 13th, 'about five of the clock in the afternoon'. They buried her under her splendid monument in All Saints Church in Derby, and there she lies undisturbed, this astonishing woman – part virago, part genius, part tycoon, part dreamer of dreams. Bess of Hardwick was a child of her age – and whatever her short-comings, whatever mistakes she made, she is worthy of an honoured place among the marvellous Elizabethans.

A note on further reading

The only modern biography of Bess is *Bess of Hardwick* by Ethel Carleton Williams, Longmans, 1959. For an older view of her see *Bess of Hardwick and her circle* by M. S. Rawson, Hutchinson, 1910.

For Arbella the choice is wider. There is *Arbella Stuart* by P. M. Handover, Eyre and Spottiswoode, 1957 and *Arabella: the life and times of Lady Arabella Seymour 1575–1615* by Ian McInnes, published by W. H. Allen, 1968. Older works are *The life and letters of Lady Arabella Stuart* by Elizabeth Cooper, 2 vols. 1866 and *The life of the Lady Arabella Stuart* by E. T. Bradley, 2 vols. 1889. (This prints many of Arbella's letters in full and covers the events of 1602–03 in considerable detail.)

The story of Catherine Grey is told in *Two Tudor portraits* by Hester Chapman, Cape, 1960. For both Arbella and Catherine see also Agnes Strickland's *Lives of the Tudor and Stuart Princesses*, Bell, 1888. Miss Strickland should be approached with some caution, but is well worth reading for her own sake.

The literature on Mary Stuart is voluminous, but the most recent full-length biography is *Mary, Queen of Scots* by Lady Antonia Fraser, Weidenfeld & Nicolson, 1969; Panther, 1970. *Mary Queen of Scots in captivity* by J. D. Leader, Bell, 1880, covers the period Mary spent in the Shrewsburys' custody, and *Mary Queen of Scots, her environment and tragedy* by T. F. Henderson, Hutchinson, 2 vols. 1905 remains the best of the older biographies.

The standard life of Elizabeth is still *Queen Elizabeth* by J. E. Neale, Cape, 1934; n.e. 1967 (in paperback). An excellent short survey of the general background is S. T. Bindoff's *Tudor England* (Pelican History of England), Penguin Books, 1950. *The Elizabethan woman* by Carroll

Camden, Cleaver-Hume Press, 1953, is interesting for social and domestic life; *Education and society in Tudor England* by Joan Simon, C.U.P. 1966 is self-explanatory and so is *Elizabethan taste* by John Buxton, Macmillan, 1963; Papermacs 1966.

Older printed sources include *Illustrations of British history* by Edmund Lodge, 3 vols. 1791 and 1838, which prints a number of the Talbot Papers, Joseph Hunter's *Hallamshire*, 1819 and, for the building of Hardwick, *Bess of Hardwick's buildings and building accounts* by Basil Stallybrass in *Archaelogia lxiv* 1913.

This, of course, is nothing like an exhaustive list. *The Calendar of State Papers relating to Scotland and Mary Queen of Scots*, the *Calendar of State Papers Spanish*, the *C.S.P. Venetian* and the *Reports of the Historical Manuscripts Commission* contain much relevant material and there are many more collections of source material.

The recent biographies mentioned above all contain detailed bibliographies and lists of references, and the invaluable *Bibliography of British history: Tudor period, 1485–1603* compiled by Conyers Read, O.U.P. 1959 is available in most reference libraries. This note is intended as no more than a brief guide to anyone interested in pursuing the subject a little further.

Index